TIME MASTERY

For Debbie —
Thanks!

John

TIME MASTERY

HOW TEMPORAL INTELLIGENCE WILL MAKE YOU

A STRONGER, MORE EFFECTIVE LEADER

JOHN CLEMENS

and

SCOTT DALRYMPLE

⁴AMACOM

American Management Association

New York • Atlanta • Brussels • Chicago • Mexico City • San Francisco
Shanghai • Tokyo • Toronto • Washington, D.C.

This publication is designed to provide accurate and authoritative
information in regard to the subject matter covered. It is sold with the
understanding that the publisher is not engaged in rendering legal,
accounting, or other professional service. If legal advice or other
expert assistance is required, the services of a competent professional
person should be sought.

Library of Congress Cataloging-in-Publication Data

Clemens, John, 1939–
      Time mastery : how temporal intelligence will make you a stronger, more
effective leader / John Clemens and Scott Dalrymple.
         p.   cm.
      Includes bibliographical references and index.
      ISBN 0-8144-0849-4
      1. Time management.   2. Leadership.   I. Dalrymple, Scott,
1967–   II. Title.

HD69 .T54C584   2005
658.4'093—dc22

2005001423

Printing number

10   9   8   7   6   5   4   3   2   1

Bill and Shirley Burgher
and
Wayne and Rhonda Dalrymple

CONTENTS

CHAPTER 5
IT'S GREEK TO ME: *CHRONOS* AND *KAIROS*   121

CHAPTER 6
TIME AS ENERGIZER   147

EPILOGUE   171

ACKNOWLEDGMENTS

MANY PEOPLE have helped make this book possible. Bill Du-charme, whose ability to ask tough questions is exceeded only by his diplomatic skill, helped transform countless ideas about the nature of temporal intelligence into reality. Bob Lorette drew upon his long and successful career in business to offer invaluable guidance. Renowned orthopedic surgeon Jim Elting helped us understand the nature of time in a busy operating room. Jane Bachman, whose extraordinary gift is a combination of temporal and emotional intelligence, quite literally improved every sentence in the manuscript while simultaneously holding our team together. Gail Michaelson, an extraordinary student, served as a valuable research assistant and conversational provocateur.

Dick Miller, newly installed president of Hartwick College, was greatly encouraging throughout the course of the project, providing near-entrepreneurial support. He has brought to the college an intellectual environment that is freshly stimulating and even fun.

Our colleagues who teach in the Hartwick Virtual Management Program—Professors John Pontius, Steve Kolenda, Katrina Zalatan, Penny Wightman, and Greg Starheim—not only contributed ideas but also tolerated our frantic schedule and our sometimes obsessive preoccupation with the emerging field of temporal intelligence.

Professor Allen C. Bluedorn, whose fascinating work on time in organizations triggered our intellectual interest in temporal intelligence, was immensely helpful. His invitation to attend an international conference on time in Fontainebleau, France, enabled us to discuss the emerging notion of temporal intelligence with international time scholars whose shoulders we now stand on—Barbara Adam, Tom Keenoy, Magid Mazen, Poppy McLeod, Steven Freeman, Pamela Meyer, Christian Noss, Jack Petranker, Ron Purser, Quy Huy, Ida Sabelis, Ram Tenkasi, Bill Torbert, and Elden Wiebe.

We want to pay special tribute to our students and to the people with whom we consult. Many of the ideas presented in this book were created and confirmed during discussions with them. As an intellectual proving ground, their contribution has been incalculable.

Carol Mann, our literary agent, not only believed in temporal intelligence from the start, but also wisely insisted on numerous rewrites. As did AMACOM's Adrienne Hickey, the editor we've been waiting for. She expressed early and enthusiastic interest in the project, fought for us when it counted, and always, always asked for 120 percent. Our kind of leader!

Finally, we acknowledge the contribution of our wives, Karyl and Connie, without whose encouragement and understanding temporal intelligence could not have been created.

TIME MASTERY

Along the way, we will share some exciting examples and concepts from business, psychology, philosophy, science, history, sports, and the arts—always with the ultimate goal of increasing your temporal intelligence and helping you become a more effective leader.

CHAPTER 1

LEADERSHIP TIME TRAVEL: PAST, PRESENT, AND FUTURE

NO OFFENSE TO OUR GRANDPARENTS, but today's demands seem so much greater than those faced by any preceding generation. Consider the following quotation from someone who knows how we feel:

> The world is too big for us. Too much going on, too many crimes, too much violence and excitement. Try as you will, you get behind in the race, in spite of yourself. It's an incessant strain, to keep pace. . . . And still, you lose ground. Science empties its discoveries on you so fast that you stagger beneath them in hopeless bewilderment. The political world is news seen so rapidly you're out of breath trying to

keep pace with who's in and who's out. Everything is high pressure. Human nature can't endure much more!

We have shown this quotation to many leaders, and invariably it resonates with them. They nod their heads in agreement, surprised that another person has so accurately captured their attitudes toward change. In the ensuing discussion, people often describe the pressure they feel living in the modern world, where the pace and magnitude of change seem truly unprecedented.

Think about it. Anyone over the age of forty remembers the days when computers were punch-card-eating behemoths the size of small homes. Now there are wearable computers. Cell phones used to be the size of briefcases, if you were lucky enough to own one; now you can easily forget one in your pants pocket and send it through the wash. Management books explain how business is changing rapidly and offer tips on how to keep up. This is to say nothing of the medical breakthroughs that have occurred in our lifetimes, or the changes in family and social structures, or political events like the collapse of the Soviet Union.

Our ancestors, impressive as they may have been, would surely crack under the pressures of our modern world. They couldn't possibly understand such rapid change.

Or could they? Read the quotation again, and this time try to identify its source. The *Los Angeles Times*? *Newsweek*? *USA Today*? Actually, it's from a lesser-known publication called the *Atlantic Journal.* Your subscription may have lapsed—since the snippet quoted here appeared in *1833*.

Americans in 1833 could be excused for believing that they had experienced some pretty remarkable and rapid changes. The Industrial Revolution was still transforming a primarily agrarian society into one based on mass production in factories, in turn fueling urbanization. The country itself was just fifty-seven years old. Adam Smith's 1776 *Wealth of Nations*, championing capitalism over mercantilism, was exactly the same age. A new transportation system, the railroad, was just beginning to appear in various parts of the country. The previous ten years had seen the advent of chloroform, the electric dynamo, and the matchstick.

Compared to that, cell phones, fax machines, and even PCs don't seem nearly as tumultuous. Our point is not that today's world *isn't* changing rapidly, but that when making such judgments, it helps to have a sense of perspective—of history. There is something calming about the knowledge that whatever problems you face this Wednesday morning, others have faced far greater challenges many times. Time masters find guidance in the past; they also find comfort in it.

▌ THE LONG NOW

Yet most individuals, organizations, and even nations seem preoccupied with the *present*. To them the future is six months, a year, two years out. Individuals tend to think of the future in terms of the next promotion, the next job, the next home improvement. Most companies think in terms of quarters, not years at all. The longest most firms plan ahead is five or *maybe* ten years. It could be argued that most governments have even shorter time horizons.

Before the turn of the millennium, computer scientist Danny Hillis—the inventor of the massively parallel computer network—began to think about our relationship with the future. He was particularly troubled by society's preoccupation with the year 2000. "Those three zeroes in the millennium form a convenient barrier," he wrote, "a reassuring boundary by which we can hold on to the present and isolate ourselves from whatever comes next." Ironically, amid all the hype about Y2K and the associated talk of the future, he saw few people pondering the true long-term fate of civilization, or of our planet.[1]

His friend Stewart Brand, founder of the *Whole Earth Catalog*, agreed. "Patience, I believe," he wrote in *Time* magazine, "is a core competency of a healthy civilization." Yet people seem to have "a pathologically short attention span," concentrating on faster ways of doing things rather than better ways. "Because we understandably pay most attention to the fast-changing elements [of civilization], we forget that the real power lies in the domains of deep, slow change."[2]

Together with like-minded people, including musician Brian Eno and futurist Esther Dyson, Hillis and Brand created the Long Now Foundation. The organization's stated goal is to create a ten-thousand-year clock, the Clock of the Long Now. Housed in a mountain in the Nevada desert, the clock will tick just once a day and chime just once a century. A cuckoo will emerge once every thousand years. The huge clock will not be powered by atomic energy, nor will it run on computer chips. In fact, it will need to be wound in order to keep moving, since Hillis is consciously designing it using very basic technology, in the event that future societies lack the knowledge to keep more complex technologies running. The works of the clock will be transparent and intuitive, just in case the clock is abandoned for some time and must be restarted. This is the result of true long-term thinking.

Of course the real goal of the clock is not to tell time for future generations, but to change the way we think about the future—to reframe our conception of time.

Brand has experience with such reframing. Back in December 1968, *Apollo 8* astronauts took the first pictures of the entire Earth from space. The beautiful blue-marble image is now a cultural icon, seen so often that we take it for granted. But many months after the photo was taken, for reasons that were unclear, the U.S. government still had not released it.

Brand started a grassroots campaign—complete with buttons and bumper stickers and the like—to force NASA to share its photo of Earth. According to Brand, this pressure led to the ultimate release of the now-famous picture. More importantly, he believes that the photo itself became a powerful symbol, reframing the way people thought about Earth. This unforgettable image made people realize that Earth is one large—and very fragile—ecosystem. By Brand's reckoning, the growth of the environmental movement after 1970 can be traced largely to the release of that photograph. Brand and Hillis hope that the Clock of the Long Now will become a similarly provocative icon, reminding us that the future is something real and important.[3]

■ TENSE TIMES

When the New York sports tabloids were focusing their journalistic lenses on the relationship between the Yankees' famed Derek Jeter and his sometime rival Alex Rodriguez, a common line of questioning was whether or not A-Rod thought Jeter was still angry about a comment he had once made. "I *thought* that was over," Rodriguez is reported to have said, triggering near-instantaneous scrutiny by a *New York Post* reporter. Might this furtive use of the past tense suggest that the rumored acrimony between the two Yankees stars was continuing unabated? Why hadn't A-Rod replied in the present tense? Why hadn't he said, "I *think* that's over."[4]

The verbs we choose reveal much about the way we think.

Verbal sleuth and computer scientist Shlomo Argamon teaches at Bar-Ilan University in Israel. Argamon has created a computer program called Winnow that he claims can determine a person's sex by analyzing that person's language patterns. After "reading" thousands of pages of text, Winnow—which has achieved an impressive 80 percent accuracy rating—has apparently learned that female writers use the present tense more often than their male counterparts.[5] Interestingly, they are also inordinate users—compared with men—of words like *for, with,* and *and,* which Argamon claims reveals their penchant for collaboration. (Males, if you haven't already guessed, expose their need for certitude by overusing determinant words such as *an, a,* and *no.*)

And there's the poignant tale of the forgotten sign, one of forty-two installed six years ago to help visitors find their way around points of interest in Lower Manhattan. Standing near the intersection of Church and Cortlandt Streets in downtown Manhattan, it still breezily asks, in a haunting present tense, "What has 200 elevators, 1,200 restrooms, more structural steel than the Verrazano Narrows Bridge?" and then goes on to declare, "Now, every weekday, 50,000 people come to work in 12 million square feet of office, hotel, and commercial space . . . where they are joined by 80,000 visitors passing through an enormous shopping mall." Ghostlike, this untimely artifact continues to tout, of course, the World Trade Center.

By such verbal mishaps, it seems, rumors are given legs, genders unwittingly revealed, and sad memories prolonged.

In writing (and in leading), time masters "get" the idea that tense counts.

Striving to achieve the "right" time perspective, the best balance of the past, the present, and the future in our lives and in our work, is how we make sense of things. An appropriate mix gives meaning to history, illuminates risks and opportunities that face us in the "now," and helps us to paint alluring pictures of things yet to come. Such attempts at sense making remind us of investors who use asset allocation models (carefully dividing their investment dollars into different categories, such as cash, bonds, stocks, and real estate) to deliver the highest returns.

When it comes to temporal portfolios, time masters face a similar, though much less rational, set of decisions. Everyone, it seems, has a profound temporal bias. Although each of us has a preferred verbal zone, we operate, think, manage, lead, and speak in all three. For simplicity's sake, we've organized these preferences into three types.

■ PAST TENSE

Traditionalists celebrate the past, the storyteller's medium. For them, the past is the foundation from which people and organizations evolve, change, and grow—the source of expertise, wisdom, and skill. Traditionalists see the past as a powerful ally, a prologue without which no agendas for the present or the future can be set. They believe that what we do today should be a continuation of what we did yesterday.

Disregard history at your peril, goes their argument, as U.S. policy makers did in 1968, when they failed to assess accurately the likelihood of a major attack by the North Vietnamese and the Vietcong in South Vietnam. Historian Stanley Karnow, who has documented America's Vietnam chapter, explained this tragic lapse. "Unfamiliar with Vietnam's past," he wrote, "very few Americans knew that one of the most famous exploits in [Vietnam's] history occurred during Tet of 1789, when the Emperor Quang Trung deceptively routed a Chinese occupation army celebrating the festival in Hanoi. Nor did they understand the Vietnamese, after centuries of internecine turmoil, were inured to duplicity."[6]

The profound danger of disregarding what has gone before is echoed by Harvard professor Ernest May, who has argued persuasively that an organization (or state) that knows its history also knows its future. When asked why anybody in business would be interested in the past, his quick retort got our attention. "Mainly," he told a reporter, "because it can reduce the number of mistakes you make."[7] After all, nothing can really be understood without hindsight, the ability to look backward, a process that has been called "retrospective sense-making." Humans, argue the Traditionalists, necessarily assume that the future will be much like the past, that the latter can provide a template or model for the former.

No wonder many *Fortune* 500 firms—Texaco, Boeing, Eli Lilly, and GE among them—have history staffs. Understanding and invoking an organization's past, it seems, may be fundamental to understanding its present and creating its future.

Yet, as anyone who has ever tried to fit a curve to historical data or has purchased a stock solely on the basis of its five-year performance knows, reverence for the past has its limitations. History may not be bunk, but it all too often *does not repeat itself.* Extrapolated futures frequently are the imaginary creatures of our own barely understood histories.

A vast body of research, however, reveals that managers overwhelmingly favor the familiar, the routine, the traditional, and the *past* over vague, uncertain visions of the future. We believe that the lopsided weight regularly given to past experiences explains many of the problems faced by organizations and individuals. The past may be an invaluable aid in coping with organizational routine, but it is woefully inadequate as a guide for innovators, adapters, and experimenters.

And then there's the sometimes cloying nostalgia that comes with overreliance on the past, those war stories that can so clearly telegraph resignation, even ennui. Listen, for example, to one-time political wunderkind Howard Dean, whose exhausted use of the past tense in speeches and interviews just before he lost the 2004 Wisconsin Democratic primary belied his "keep your chin up" mettle.

"The campaign *was* fueled by an intense desire to change presidents and make sure that George Bush *went* back to Crawford," he told an understandably cheerless audience. "The reason this campaign *did* so well pre-Iowa is because I *was* the only candidate willing to stand up to George Bush . . ." he continued. All this was concluded anti-climactically with the words "A lot of new things *have happened* because of this campaign. We *did get* to put some spine in the Democratic Party again after an absence of that" [emphasis ours].[8]

Who wouldn't agree that there *was* no future for this political campaign?

▮ PRESENT TENSE

We call our second temporal group *Contemporaries*, people who operate almost exclusively in the present. "Don't worry about tomorrow," is their mantra. "Just get through the day!" Contemporaries have been hugely helped not only by time management courses and self-help gurus, but also by none other than Peter Drucker, whose legendary musings about management and leadership include the assertion that decisions exist only in the *present*. He has suggested that his readers and clients lop off the past as a useful context for decision making, as he thinks it too likely to dampen creativity and change. Contemporaries eschew the past while enthusiastically embracing the present.

Patrick O'Brian, creator of the story behind the film *Master and Commander* and author of a series of novels about the British Navy during the Napoleonic Wars, appreciated the ubiquity of the present. He has one of his two principal characters, the naturalist-turned-seafarer Stephen Maturin, unravel this human affinity for the present:

> I have watched [sailors] attentively, and find that they are more unsuited to life than men of any other calling whatsoever. I propose the following reason for this: the sailor, at sea (his proper element), lives in the present. There is nothing he can do about the past at all; and, having regard to the uncertainty of the omnipotent ocean and the weather, very little about the future. This, I may say in passing, accounts for the common tar's improvidence. The officers spend their lives fighting against this attitude on the part of the men—persuading them to tighten ropes, to belay and so on, against a vast series of contingencies; but the offi-

cers, being as sea-borne as the rest, do their task with a half conviction: from this arises uneasiness of mind, and hence the vagaries of those in authority. Sailors will provide against a storm tomorrow, or even in a fortnight's time; but for them the remoter possibilities are academic, unreal. They live in the present, I say.[9]

He may have been right. Stanford University professor James March, famed for his study of how people and organizations deal with information, considers the present to be a kind of organizational safe haven. It is a temporal zone in which time-tested routines can be perfected, existing methods sharpened, and current procedures refined. Driven by this present sense of time, many managers focus single-mindedly on the clear and unambiguous *now*: doing the same things, only better; reaping value from what is already known; defending beaten paths; and quite often unwittingly empowering the bureaucracy. Think efficiency, productivity, routine, and repetition.

March calls this living and thinking in the present tense "exploitation."[10]

You concentrate on your current core competencies. You nurture growth in areas in which you have demonstrated competence. You focus on tactics. You play zero-sum games.

We're reminded of the kind of over-the-top market share battles that are waged regularly by consumer products companies. The temporal moment for these multimillion-dollar confrontations is the A. C. Nielsen Company's weekly data-gathering cycle. Launch a display promotion for your new soft drink product in ten cities, and seven days later you know whether or not you clobbered the competition. That's real time!

No wonder an obsessive commitment to the present can get businesses into a lot of trouble. Not only has it given birth to the economic imperative "maximize shareholder value right now, or we'll get someone who can," but it has also caused a sea change in the way people invest. Holding periods for stocks, once a respectable five years or so, have plummeted to less than six months, transforming true investors into speculators. CEOs, told to "live for today," work only to make Wall Street's numbers, often shunning long-term investments in favor of short-term gains. Quarterly earnings per share (about as present tense as you can get in corporate finance) replaces all other metrics as a measure of a company's health.

Contemporaries bring to mind an ancient tale about the hedgehog. A simple animal, the hedgehog seems to spend its entire life living only in the now. Not at all fast and apparently possessed of no sense of strategy, little guile, and no long-term plan other than to survive and to feed its family, it seems doomed to extinction. Yet it routinely defeats its natural enemy, the fox, by using its one defense—when threatened, it rolls up into a ball and projects sharp spikes in every direction. As the story goes, "The fox knows many things, but the hedgehog knows one big thing." That "one big thing," according to philosopher and historian Isaiah Berlin, consists of a coherent and consistent vision coupled with tenacious single-mindedness. No wonder the word *hedgehog* has come to mean "a well-fortified military stronghold."

∎ FUTURE TENSE

Finally, there are the *Futurists*, people who have weaned themselves from both past and present. They live their lives in the future tense, acting and thinking ahead. They have discovered the joys (and the good business sense) of imagining and envisioning the future, and as a result they have rejected the limitations of current routine. They choose instead to create innovative solutions and new scenarios. Dissatisfied with their existing core competencies, they invest resources in creating new ones. Tired of being merely derivative, they seek genius, new templates, new matrices.

Their focus is strategy. Futurists find ambiguity and inconsistency tolerable, even alluring. Rule breakers rather than rule makers, they are unabashed iconoclasts who change industries and markets. Consider, for example, Dell's breakthrough exploration into the heart of the computer industry, where conventional wisdom insisted that a product must be produced before it is sold, lest distribution costs become prohibitive. Dell's seemingly wacky futuristic vision—to assemble the product only after it had been sold—was an important basis for the company's dramatic success in the personal computer business.

Dell is an example of another ancient myth, that of the wily fox: moving beyond the present on many levels at once; breaking out of its comfort zone; innovating aggressively; and possessing multiple strategies, many agendas, myriad challenges, and unknown potentials. A sense of futurity drives much of what happens at Microsoft as well, where experimentation—whether successful or not—is encouraged and rewarded. Microsoft employees, understandably, are famously persistent explorers for whom every failure is a step on the path to success.

Avid rock climber and best-selling author Jim Collins knows about these steps into an uncertain future. His whole life has been about developing his skills as a climber. It all started when, as a senior in high school, he discovered that Stanford University's buildings could be climbed between classes. Since then, he's been applying the lessons learned on rock faces to almost everything, including leadership.

Take Collins's climb up Genesis, a forbidding, 100-foot red rock located in Colorado's Eldorado Canyon. Nobody had yet free-climbed it. Collins had studied it closely, watching others make the try. Finally, noticing that climbs thought to be impossible by one generation frequently became "not that hard" for those who attempted them several generations later, he decided to climb *into the future*. Collins projected the climb out fifteen years, asking, "What will climbers think about this challenge then?"

His study of the history of rock climbing answered back: "It'll be routine!"

Collins immediately time-traveled into the future. He changed his calendar, advancing it fifteen years. He pretended that it was not 1979 but 1994. He got himself out of the present and into the future. As he tells it, "It caused quite a sensation and confused many of the best climbers of the day. They were still climbing in 1979, whereas I had psychologically transported myself to 1994."[11] It should come as no surprise that Collins ultimately conquered Genesis.

Time masters share Collins's capacity to explore by putting their minds into the future tense. They do this by telescoping years ahead, acting as if they were living in a new and unknown world, one that has already been transformed. What was once unimaginable becomes eminently doable.

■ TEMPORAL GOLDEN MEAN

The key, of course, is to find the temporal golden mean, that right proportion of past, present, and future that optimizes leadership. Each must get its due. Underlying patterns cannot be recognized without the benefit of the historian's eye. Projecting forward must begin from a platform constructed in the present. Without a sense of history, there is no basis for making decisions that affect the future.

Too much exploitation, simply operating in the present tense and refining what we already know or do, results in what economists call "lock-in." This creates a kind of commercial inbreeding that results in everything from unsafe cars to the oh-so-slow QWERTY typewriter keyboard—originally designed to prevent keys from jamming, but a useless relic in the age of the personal computer.

Conversely, obsession with exploration, with moving beyond existing knowledge, structure, and action, means increased risk, less efficient use of resources, and frequent failure. Here the *Challenger* and *Columbia* space shuttle disasters come to mind.

■ TIME TO THINK ABOUT THE FUTURE

Ask a group of executives which is most important to a firm—the past, the present, or the future—and most likely a clever person will offer, "All three." If forced to choose, though, chances are that most people will say, "The future." The present is crucial, they point out. But true leaders must think about the future, create a compelling vision of the future, and lead people to it. Leadership 101 stuff.

And good stuff.

But in our experience, many leaders don't walk the talk. To prove it, we have developed a simple but powerful exercise to gauge the future orientation of leaders. We call it Verb-Audit.

We often ask groups of leaders to complete a simple task: *Write a paragraph about your company*. That's all. We offer no further instructions. We allow a reasonable period of time, say ten or twelve minutes, for people to complete their paragraphs. They scribble away, some more eloquently than others.

Then the fun begins. Participants read their own paragraphs to themselves, or perhaps swap with a partner, paying particular attention to *verbs*. We ask them to circle all of the verbs in their paragraphs. Next, we ask them to categorize each verb as past, present, or future tense. When the categorization is complete, we ask participants to count the number of past, present, and future verbs they used in their paragraphs.

A simple exercise, with often powerful results.

Since the participants have only a few minutes, the paragraphs usually aren't very polished. But that's why the exercise works; people are writing their top-of-mind thoughts, with little time for self-editing. Here is a composite example:

> Pinnacle Corporation is based in Buffalo, New York. We have 850 employees and operate two shifts year-round. We manufacture hiking boots for men and women. Our main product is the GripMaster line, but we also sell quite a few ClimbCaptains. We distribute in thirteen countries. We sell mainly through specialty sporting goods retailers, but we also have some high-end department store accounts. Our advertising is primarily in specialty outdoor-life magazines. We were founded in 1936 by Hugo Popov, who always insisted on top-quality materials and workmanship. Today, Pinnacle is one of the most respected names in the industry. Our market research consistently shows that customers

buy Pinnacle for its quality. We aren't the most stylish hiking boot out there, but we appeal to the serious hiker. Our sales last year were $35 million. We are adding the Johnson's Sporting Goods chain to our group of distributors. With any luck, we will reach $40 million next year.

Not a masterpiece of literature, perhaps, but pretty typical. Now look at the paragraph again, this time paying attention to verb tense. We'll underline all past-tense verbs, mark all present-tense verbs in bold, and mark all future-tense verbs in italics:

Pinnacle Corporation **is** based in Buffalo, New York. We **have** 850 employees and **operate** two shifts year-round. We **manufacture** hiking boots for men and women. Our main product **is** the GripMaster line, but we also **sell** quite a few ClimbCaptains. We **distribute** in thirteen countries. We **sell** mainly through specialty sporting goods retailers, but we also **have** some high-end department store accounts. Our advertising **is** primarily in specialty outdoor-life magazines. We were founded in 1936 by Hugo Popov, who always insisted on top-quality materials and workmanship. Today, Pinnacle **is** one of the most respected names in the industry. Our market research consistently **shows** that customers **buy** Pinnacle for its quality. We **aren't** the most stylish hiking boot out there, but we **appeal** to the serious hiker. Our sales last year were $35 million. We **are** adding the Johnson's Sporting Goods chain to our group of distributors. With any luck, we *will* reach $40 million next year.

The final tally for this paragraph: three past-tense verbs, sixteen present-tense verbs, and one future-tense verb. This writer is clearly focused on the here and now, with a slight nod to the past and very little interest in the future. This may sound harsh—after all, the poor author had just a few minutes to write. Yet in our experience, this quick exercise reveals much about what a person finds important.

And the truth is, VerbAudit nearly always shows an *overwhelming preoccupation with the present.* The typical result is 80 percent present-tense verbs, 15 percent past-tense, and just 5 percent future-tense. These figures might be fine in some cases, say for a how-to guide or to describe the current football season. But for corporate leaders who have been asked to "write a paragraph about your company," they are often disconcerting.

This exercise can reveal much about leadership; sometimes how people *react* to the exercise reveals even more.

We once conducted VerbAudit with the senior management team of a large, household-name corporation. As usual, the results betrayed a very clear *present* orientation. When describing their company, very few of the executives wrote about potential strategic alliances, or eventual expansion, or truly long-range financial goals. They were caught up in the company's day-to-day problems. Their thought processes were mired in the present. They were *managing* the firm, not *leading* it into the future.

The senior executive at the seminar (whose own paragraph was almost completely stuck in the present) was simply aghast. Who, he asked aloud, was thinking about the future? Five years, ten years, twenty years out and beyond? Confronted with this disturbing reality, the executive vowed that the leadership team would change the way it thought about time. The future would be ever-present, so to speak.

Not all people, however, have the same type of reaction.

We used the same exercise with regional managers for a major financial services firm. Each of these managers was responsible for a multimillion-dollar business unit and hundreds of employees.

As usual, the exercise revealed a strong preoccupation with the present. After pointing this out, we stood ready for the kind of temporal epiphany we had seen so often before. Instead, there was silence. "Do we have a problem here?" we prodded. No response. The managers remained decidedly underwhelmed; if the truth be told, many of them thought it just about the dumbest exercise they had ever seen.

Finally, one of them spoke up. "You don't seem to understand our business," he said. "I live in the present. I just don't have time to think about the future." This from a high-six-figure regional manager with P&L responsibility for growing a business unit. Nearly everyone in the room agreed with him. They didn't have time to think about the future. That was somebody else's job, presumably at headquarters. Maybe the CEO was doing it. Isn't that what she's paid for?

These managers reminded us of goalies in ice hockey, skillfully deflecting the various pucks flying at them from all directions. Now, we have nothing against goalies. Certainly organizations, like hockey teams, need good goalies. But goalies are by definition reactive. They engage in a bit of future thinking—trying to predict precisely where the opposition's forward is likely to shoot the puck, for instance—but they tend to think, quite appropriately, in the present.

The problem is that in organizations, it's often good goalies who are promoted to leadership positions. After all, they got the team this far, right? And even after being promoted, many such people continue to think and act like goalies. Temporally, they remain preoccupied with the present, even though they now have a much broader scope of responsibility. To continue the hockey analogy, these leaders need to start thinking like team presidents or general managers: assessing overall team needs, managing future draft picks, scouting young players, planning for a new arena—in other words, thinking about the long term.

The former goalies know this, of course. They understand, logically, that they need to do these things. They may vow to think more strategically, to plan and think about the future. They may even attend leadership seminars to that effect. Then the cell phone rings. And there are thirty-seven messages on the BlackBerry. And today's calendar is completely booked, from 7 a.m. to 7 p.m. And the Fresno office manager quits.

Inevitably, in the face of such current pressures, the innate goalie starts to take over. The cell phone is answered and the problem is successfully deflected—a save. The thirty-seven BlackBerry messages are variously read, responded to, and ignored as appropriate—thirty-seven more saves. The Fresno debacle is resolved—a spectacular save! In fact, it may all be a truly impressive display of goal tending. But is it leadership?

In fairness to folks like these, the problem is often one of corporate culture.

If managers are rewarded solely for the number of saves made, for reactive resolutions to problems, then top executives need to evaluate the temporal cues they are sending their subordinates. Incentive systems may need to be realigned to reflect new temporal priorities. If you want your leaders to be thinking about the future at least 25 percent of the time, then at least 25 percent of their incentive packages had better be directed toward future-oriented goals like long-term strategic planning. Otherwise, the best lip service in the world is not going to pry people away from the day's minor crises.

And if your leaders don't have time to think about the future, then there may not be one.

■ PROFITING FROM THE PAST, PRESENT, AND FUTURE

General Electric is the most discussed, envied, and imitated firm in corporate America. Its annual revenues of $135 billion place it fifth on the *Fortune* 500; its market capitalization of more than $300 billion makes it the most valuable company in the United States. GE's 300,000 employees make everything from light bulbs to jet engines, and make money doing it—$15 billion in 2003. The company is perennially at or near the top of any survey of America's most admired corporations. Unless you've been living in a yurt for twenty years, you know that from 1981 to 2001, GE was led by the inimitable Jack Welch, who (with the possible exception of Berkshire Hathaway's Warren Buffett) has been the most quoted business leader of our time. Welch has been called "legendary," "the master CEO," and "the world's greatest business leader" (and that's just in the titles of books written about him).[12]

Welch's track record at GE was extremely impressive. He brought to the company an adaptive, high-energy, take-no-prisoners leadership style. His famous admonition to GE leaders was that the company's business units were to be number one or two in their respective industries, or else the company would pull out of those industries. He concentrated on shareholder value, rather than revenue, as the benchmark for success. And this strategy clearly worked: Under his leadership, GE added scores of billions of dollars to its market capitalization.

But impressive as he was, the story of Jack Welch is not the story of General Electric. In fact, the company's roots go all the way back to Thomas Edison, who in 1879, after more than a thousand failed attempts, finally succeeded in creating a long-lasting lightbulb (at the time, long-lasting meant about thirteen hours). GE's CEO from 1892 to 1922, Charles Coffin, was the one who methodically built the company's electrical equipment business. Owen Young, CEO from 1922 to 1940 (and *Time*'s Man of the Year in 1929), worried that GE was becoming a generic corporate giant; in order to make the GE name resonate for average Americans, he led the company's charge into home appliances. Charles Wilson (1940–1950) led GE through the challenges of World War II and positioned the company for the boom years to follow. Ralph Cordiner (1950–1963), a student of Frederick Taylor's scientific management, was the first to break GE into separate business units. Fred Borch (1963–1972) invested heavily in aircraft engines, which today make up a large part of GE's $15 billion a year transportation business. Reginald Jones (1972–1981) concentrated on improving GE's financial health, positioning the company for future growth.

Then came Jack Welch, who realized that growth in a big way.

Over the years, GE scientists invented the x-ray tube, the tungsten light, magnetic resonance imaging (MRI), and the solid-state lasers used in most copiers and fax machines. Of the companies in the 1896 Dow Jones index, only GE remains.

GE's current CEO, Jeff Immelt, is acutely aware of the company's rich heritage, and it shapes the way he thinks about GE's present and its future. He understands that his predecessors made an effort to plan ahead—sometimes decades ahead. They appreciated the past, but they were not limited by it. In fact, when Reginald Jones handed over the reins to Jack Welch, he encouraged Welch to "blow it up," to change the company if that was what it took to succeed. Welch told Immelt the same thing.

Immelt obviously listened. The environment he faces is different even from that faced by Welch just a few years ago, and Immelt is planning for change. He is moving GE out of many of the financial services businesses that Welch pioneered. He is making major changes to head off growing competition from China, shuffling GE's portfolio of businesses such that Chinese companies can't compete with GE. "Ten years out, 90 percent of our company's earnings will have no competition from China. Eighty percent of our businesses will be selling to China," he announced in 2003. In addition, he has increased funding for research and development, particularly for projects at GE's Global Research Center—the site of the company's most significant breakthroughs over the past hundred years.

Some of Immelt's moves are likely to have a negative impact on GE's earnings for a number of years. But this is one leader with a high degree of temporal intelligence; he doesn't seem worried. "I run a company that's 125 years old," he told *Fortune* magazine in 2004. "There's going to be someone after me, just as there was someone before me."[13]

Immelt, it seems, has his eye on the past, the present, *and* the future.

■ HOW YOU CAN APPLY TEMPORAL INTELLIGENCE

When you wrap the present with the past and the future, you tap into powerful resources that can help make extraordinary things happen. Suddenly people who were mired in the now become liberated. For the first time, they have a coherent, and much richer, temporal context for their work and their leadership. They know where they have been, and they see clearly where they are going.

Here are some ways you can escape the tyranny of the present:

- Don't get mired in the short term. Stop worrying about maximizing shareholder value right now, and focus instead on the long-term future and creating long-term value. Pay for company performance, not for stock performance. That's the way to build wealth.

- Time travel. While bidding for the military's $19 billion Joint Strike Fighter (JSF) program, Lockheed-Martin's Tom Burbage attacked a morale problem by throwing a dinner for hundreds of JSF team members. He then unveiled jumbo-sized mock-ups of business magazines and newspapers. Above pictures of the new fighter, headlines proudly proclaimed "Lockheed's Joint Strike Fighter Takes Off" and "How Did They Do It?" Each was dated a full four years into the future.

- Practice the art of "what if?" Constantly create fresh, new scenarios of future possibilities and new business models in order to create, rather than react to, the marketplace.

■ Ride your heritage. You don't need to visit a HOG
   rally to recognize that Harley-Davidson lives its tra-
   ditions. As the company's marketing vice president
   told *Fast Company* in August 2004, "the founding
   fathers actually seep out of the walls here."[14]
   Harley-Davidson's competitive advantage is not
   product quality or innovative design; it's history.

■ Backcast. Paint a futuristic picture in your mind of
   how you want things to look a year, two years, five
   years from now. Buy a calendar and change all the
   dates so that 2005 becomes, say, 2010. Make a reverse timetable showing key events that you
   would like to see happen. This, not some dusty
   plaque on the wall, is the way to harness the
   power of a corporate vision.

■ Maintain a sense of temporal perspective. Whatever challenges you face a week from Thursday,
   know that mankind has faced, and overcome,
   much greater obstacles in its history—and will do
   so in the future. Calm down. Think about it: Will
   this crisis matter to you twenty years from now?

CHAPTER 2

GOING WITH THE FLOW

LIKE THE REST OF US, time masters live in the perpetual white water of turbulent schedules, caroming from one meeting to the next, their days filled with a hodgepodge of different roles—hosting a client dinner, taking a phone call, mentoring a colleague, communicating critical information, deciding who gets what. They exemplify the multitasking leaders who are sometimes called "polychronic."[1] They engage in many activities at the same time: Their open office doors encourage people to poke their heads in when they feel like it, phones are casually answered in the midst of other tasks, priorities are continually juggled, time is compressed, and decisions are high-speed. Activities overlap, dovetail, and disrupt one another.

But time masters don't schedule every minute of the day, nor do they live slavishly by the lines and entries in their calendars. Unlike a fellow airline passenger whom we once observed intently filling out not one, but *three* calendars, they seem to understand that such detailed to-do lists can cause the really important priorities of the day to fall through the temporal cracks. Ironically, this kind of temporal obsession *takes* time. One study, in fact, found that as many as 30 percent of list makers spend more time managing their lists than completing what's on them![2]

Sure, time masters make lists, but they are not nearly as insistent on those lists as dedicated time managers are. More than likely, time masters enumerate those things that need to get done *presently.* (The French, who know something about the good life, have the perfect phrase for this: *Tôt ou tard,* which means "sooner or later.") Time masters are not inveterate slicers and dicers of time, habitual calendarizers wed to the principle that time is divisible into bits and pieces. They are less interested than most in pinning it down, or in imposing their own personal blueprint on the stream of time. They seem to know that so-called prioritized activities often turn out to be those that are pressing but easy, and that interruptions (deplored by time management consultants) are so much a part of the job that they must, perhaps ironically, be planned for.

Time masters refuse to divide up what is in truth a continuous flow. They perceive time as seamless, indivisible, like the single unending edge of a Möbius strip. (That's the loop whose twisted contours both frustrate and fascinate as its back transforms itself into its front, and its end inexplicably becomes its starting point.) Time masters go through their day making time when needed, joining diverse experiences into a meaningful pattern, creating order in a chaotic, fragmented world. Unwitting temporal iconoclasts, they seek continuity, sensing that life—both personal and organizational—is a process, a series of gradual changes. Like all good narratives, it is not composed of short episodic takes, but instead is a progression of long tracking shots.

A former president of our college, a social psychologist by training, possessed a high degree of temporal intelligence. We once attended a meeting with him to get his perspective on the future of our academic program. It was a very pleasant conversation. He was amiable and attentive, and he seemed quite satisfied with our plans and our strategy.

But as we were leaving, he changed everything.

"You know," he said, "you have an excellent program. You can keep it the way it is, or you can develop it into a truly great undergraduate program. It's up to you. Thanks for dropping by."

We didn't immediately grasp the full meaning of that enigmatic send-off. We kept thinking, pondering, wondering what he meant. Then, suddenly, the lights went on. The message was clear. We *would* transform our program. We *would* make it world class. And with the help of our colleagues, we started a journey, spending the next few years doing just that.

Looking back, we realized that we had left this seemingly indecisive encounter shaking our heads in confusion. Yet what had seemed so ambiguous was really the building of flow, creativity, ownership, and continuity.

We've observed this phenomenon so many times that we have given it a name, the *hallway double-take*, that sought-after but rarely achieved delayed reaction that means that people are processing, absorbing, and beginning to get what just went on. They haven't closed their minds, they've opened them.

Temporally intelligent leaders, we were beginning to sense, don't believe in endings. Instead, they keep discussions going. They don't buy into the platitudes that insist that they must always go for the close, set priorities, summarize action steps, assign responsibilities, *finish*. Instead, they often (and purposely) leave things open, even ambiguous. Even conventional meeting closes are frequently shunned, in the belief that tying up all the loose ends can often ruin what has gone before.

They know that process is often as important as action, and that (as one of our savvy colleagues put it, paraphrasing Yogi Berra) "the meeting doesn't end until the meeting ends." And they carefully evaluate how the next block of time should be invested: deciding, for example, to continue with an impromptu but productive conversation in the hall even if it means rearranging the rest of their day. They treat their calendar as suggestive rather than definitive, a work in progress. They know that the moments spent in each meeting, each conversation, and each daily time commitment are important links in a means-end chain. They build connections and synergies into everything they do, ensuring that seemingly unrelated meetings, discussions, and conversations converge rather than diverge.

■ ENEMIES OF CONTINUITY

Time masters do battle with discontinuity . . . continuously. They are wary of technology that emphasizes efficiency over effectiveness. Take, for example, presentation software like Microsoft's PowerPoint. Now installed in more than three hundred million computers throughout the world, this killer app has changed the way we talk, think, persuade, and even decide. Having sent grammatical conventions like paragraphs, pronouns, and transitions into oblivion, PowerPoint handily reduces almost everything into those now-famous bullet points, which have, as *New Yorker* magazine pundit Ian Parker puts it, "shepherded [the user] toward a staccato, summarizing frame of mind."[3]

But the shape-shifting imprint of PowerPoint's editorial knife doesn't end there. By eradicating pronouns and encouraging the passive voice, it destroys intellectual accountability and ownership of the very ideas it seeks to advance, making it a marvelous device for avoiding responsibility. Convenience trumps quality, content becomes shallow, and the medium itself too often becomes the message. And, most importantly, the audience doesn't see the presenter's flow of thought. As Stanford professor Clifford Nass, whom Parker interviewed, put it, "What you miss is the process. The classes I remember most, the professors I remember most, were the ones where you could watch how they thought."[4]

Time masters also have a healthy skepticism toward deadlines, those ubiquitous tools of time management and creators of discontinuity. They know, of course, that deadlines occasionally have their place. Delicate negotiations, for example, may dictate the establishment of a zero hour in order to neutralize the other party's delaying tactics. Yet when working with people on their teams, time masters often shun deadlines because hard stops shut down creativity. (The word *deadline* originally referred to a mark drawn around the perimeter of a prison, beyond which inmates would be shot.)

Research on the effects of deadlines confirms what time masters sense. When it comes to encouraging breakthrough thinking and innovation, due dates often don't work. "When creativity is under the gun," writes Harvard professor Teresa Amabile, who with her colleagues studies the effects of time pressure on innovative thinking, "it usually ends up getting killed." She and her colleagues found that the use of deadlines and high levels of time pressure put people on a treadmill that caused them to feel distracted, resulted in more meetings, and fragmented the workday. Put simply, the higher the time pressure and the greater the use of deadlines, the lower the creativity—and the continuity.[5]

■ CONTINUITY IN ART AND MUSIC

We learned a great deal about continuity in a small museum in Madrid, where we spent the better part of a morning studying a single piece of art, Picasso's monumental *Guernica*. The huge mural, which documents the moment in April 1937 when fascist bombs ravaged a tiny Basque village, starkly reveals the horrible devastation of war. An injured horse screams, its tongue protruding grotesquely. A grief-stricken woman mourns, her dead baby heavy in her arms. A bare lightbulb dangles incongruously. It seemed clear to us that this painting, with its fragmented images and stark planes, was about destruction, about the sudden change from life to death, about *discontinuity*.

But a museum guide helped us to see the subtle connections in *Guernica*. He patiently showed us—two art novices—how Picasso's hard-edged blacks and whites meld into ambiguous grays, creating curious shapes. He explained that the haunting lightbulb, hanging like a beacon at the apex of the mural's triangular form, illuminates what art critic and poet Eli Siegel called the *"continuity* of life, of death, and reality."[6] It changed the way we thought about art, and about time. We became convinced that time mastery, like great art, insists on continuity.

Wynton Marsalis would agree. Performing at the Village Vanguard, a venerable New York jazz club, the legendary musician was playing a solo version of the Victor Young romantic ballad "I Don't Stand a Ghost of a Chance with You." When at last Marsalis reached the final sad bars of the piece, the room fell silent, the audience stunned by his genius.

Until, that is, a cell phone rang out, bringing the performance to a clumsy halt.

But Marsalis was not about to be upstaged by a mere cell phone. After a brief pause, he continued, replaying the simple four-note sequence several times. Then he went on with increasingly brilliant improvised adaptations of the theme. *Atlantic Monthly* music critic David Hajdu, who was in the audience that night, described this moment of musical continuity: "The audience slowly came back to him. In a few minutes he resolved the improvisation—which had changed keys once or twice and throttled down to a ballad tempo—and ended up exactly where he had left off: 'with . . . you . . .' The ovation was tremendous."[7]

Continuity is a true art.

■ FROM CAUSAL TIME TO FLOW TIME

Temporal intelligence pioneers Ron Purser and Jack Petranker would agree. Purser, a management professor at San

Francisco State University, and Petranker, founding director of the Center for Creative Inquiry in Berkeley, California, are convinced that the nearly universal treatment of time as discontinuous—yes, those day-timers and calendars again—seriously inhibits our ability to plan and manage change intelligently.[8]

Purser and Petranker believe that time is too often seen as one-dimensional, a kind of rudimentary measuring device that is organized and indexed, chopped and separated, into equal units such as minutes, hours, or days. Its linearity—from past to present to future—neatly translates into everything from those fifteen-minute chunks so common in pocket calendars to the time lines that celebrate important dates in the trajectory of organizations, institutions, or ideas. Events are erroneously understood as a series of frozen moments, or "still shots"—static states in linear succession.

Things become so precisely organized, so seemingly comprehensible, in fact, that causality (the comforting notion that whatever arises in the future has its origin in the past) is simply assumed. Priorities are scrupulously set. Lists (and more lists) are created. Activities are assigned to those time slots on the calendar. Thus laid out neatly fore and aft, the chaos of the day is vanquished, organized into manageable bits that one simply works through, step by step, *seriatim.* Purser and Petranker call this "causal time."

Their fascinating alternative? "Flow time."

To put this into business terms, consider some ordinary financial statements. Flow time is to causal time what cash flow (yes, that's cash *flow*) is to the balance sheet. Cash flow (sometimes cartoonishly portrayed as a faucet pouring water into a bucket with a hole in the bottom) does in fact ebb and flow like the tide, constantly revealing where the money comes from and where it goes. The cash flow statement does things no other financial report can, revealing not only how much income was made, but whether operations generated cash or used cash, what assets were acquired, and how everything was financed. Its essence is continuity. Its value is its marvelous comprehensiveness and rich narrative.

The balance sheet, on the other hand, is a report so static that it quite literally freezes time—it is accurate "as of December 31, 2005," but it is incapable of dealing with periods like "December 1 to December 31." Its meticulously balanced assets, liabilities, and net worth provide a telling snapshot of a business at a specific (and quite discontinuous) moment in time. Balance sheets have their place, to be sure. But they're a flash in the pan compared to the cash flow statement.

It's this kind of continuity that drives the world of futures trading, a profession in which risk and time converge. "The essence of risk," one trader told a reporter, "is not that it *is* happening, but that it *might be* happening." Without continuity, there can be no risk. What's more, the two have a curious effect on each other. "Sometimes, like the tide," the trader said, "it reverses the normal flow of temporal relationships. Instead of the past determining the future, risk causes what might happen in the future to determine the present."[9] This process, which financial types call *present value*, enables the flow to go both ways.

Another perspective on flow was first studied by Mihaly Csikszentmihalyi, who teaches management and psychology at the renowned Drucker School of Management at Claremont Graduate University in southern California. Csikszentmihalyi defines *flow* as a state of concentration so focused that it amounts to absolute absorption in an activity.

Cruising sailors, those individualists who (like one of us)

leave so-called successful careers to make years of sailing a central part of their lives, exemplify the flow model. There's challenge and danger and only intrinsic reward—piloting an ancient twenty-six-foot wooden sloop around the western Mediterranean for five years yields neither fame nor money. But it marvelously reorganized a life crammed with the trivia and detail of "normal" society into a continuous flow experience.

Mountain climbers, too, routinely report a sense of the uninterrupted continuity that occurs at high altitudes. During the ascent phase, as one climber puts it, "the present [is] always filled with the future. Reaching the summit abruptly turns all of this into the past. And with every step down towards the valley and towards human civilization, you get an inkling that, after all, the summit you just scaled is only *pre-summit* to your next one."[10]

It all got started when Csikszentmihalyi was climbing his own summit, working on his doctoral dissertation. Watching art students create paintings, he was intrigued by what he saw: an absolute focus on the task at hand that transcended the moment. The students seemed to be entirely involved, concentrated, and absorbed. They did not stop to eat, they did not become fatigued, they missed appointments, and their awareness of time disappeared. They forgot themselves and became lost in the activity. When asked about this unusual behavior, several of the students answered by describing a sense of flow. They said it felt as if they were being carried away by a current, that everything was moving smoothly and without effort.

The key ingredient seemed to be *the ability to match challenge with capability*. Flow aficionados call this the "challenge-skills" balance. It is familiar to anyone who has prepared to hit a golf ball on the first tee or has jockeyed for position before a jump ball. There's a feeling of nervousness because no one wants to start out with a mistake. And there's a sense of eagerness because you're well prepared. Csikszentmihalyi puts it this way:

> When challenges are high and personal skills are used to the utmost, we experience this rare state of consciousness. The first symptom of flow is a narrowing of attention on a clearly defined goal. We feel involved, concentrated, absorbed. We know what must be done, and we get immediate feedback as to how well we are doing. The tennis player knows after each shot whether the ball actually went where she wanted it to go; the pianist knows after each stroke of the keyboard whether the notes sound like they should. Even a usually boring job, once the challenges are brought into balance with the person's skills and the goals are clarified, can begin to be exciting and involving.[11]

Flow, in other words, is much more than a fad. It can change the nature of work. When you're in flow, you're fully absorbed rather than bored, so involved in an activity that nothing else seems to matter. You have a deep sense of satisfaction rather than ennui and indifference. You lose track of time.

Every action, movement, and thought follows inevitably from the previous one. Your whole being is involved, and you're at the edge, using your skills to the limit. There is a clear goal, feedback is accurate and immediate, the degree of challenge is roughly matched by one's skills, and the activity is worth doing for its own sake. For many people, these optimal experiences are the high points in their lives.

■ APPLYING CONTINUITY

Even competitive strategist Michael Porter of Harvard has begun going with the flow. Having witnessed a decade-long decline in strategic planning caused by managers' near-maniacal focus on execution and implementation, he now proclaims that only strategy can create a sustainable competitive advantage. There's nothing new about this, of course. But there *is* something refreshingly innovative in Porter's realization that strategy, if it is to work, must be continuous.

Citing Southwest Airlines' thirty-year history of serving price-conscious travelers with reliable but limited service, he concludes that "strategy must have continuity. It can't be constantly reinvented. Strategy is about the basic values you're trying to deliver to customers. . . . That positioning . . . is where continuity needs to be strongest."[12]

Not surprisingly, flow—think of it as *applied continuity*—has become a critical part of such diverse business endeavors as market segmentation and web site design. Vanderbilt University's Donna Hoffman and Thomas Novak, for example, who study consumer behavior in commercial online environments, have enlisted Csikszentmihalyi's brainchild in their effort to make surfing the World Wide Web more compelling. Consumers, they have found, are so engrossed in piloting their way though the Internet that they are—you guessed it—*in flow*, unwittingly filtering out everything else around them. Hoffman and Novak describe this never-never land as a place where "self-consciousness disappears, the consumer's sense of time becomes distorted, and the state of mind arising as a result of achieving flow on the Web is extremely gratifying."[13] And profitable. Web-based e-commerce is now a $50 billion industry.

As with those art students whom Csikszentmihalyi observed, the flow that occurs while surfing the Web is the result of matching challenge with capability. Perhaps this explains why trendy web sites like Orbitz.com and FT.com (that's the *Financial Times*) occasionally welcome you to the web site not with a hot travel deal or the latest business story, but with an online putting contest or the opportunity to play a round of golf in a simulated Ryder Cup tournament.

Why do they do this? Because their web site designers want to get you into the flow, totally concentrated on the strongest marketing tool they have—the web site. They know that adroitly balancing challenge with capability (the golf is not *that* difficult) does wonders to focus your online attention. Surprising the customer with a game of digital golf as a web site gambit means more continuity and more business.

But applied continuity does more than simply bring in revenue. It alters the fundamental ways in which we think about business. Free-enterprise capitalism and the well-founded belief that only the fittest survive have nurtured the conviction that business is usually a zero-sum game. One organization's gain is another's loss. For every winner, there is a loser. Business is a chess game with only one victorious player. Share-of-market battles model this imperative perfectly. A 2 percent gain in share for one firm must, necessarily, translate into a loss for someone else. Checkmate. Game over.

◼ COOPERATING TO COMPETE

Maybe not. It turns out that the game does not have to end. It's better, we discovered from some of our more imaginative time masters, to *keep the contest going.* And, on occasion, to let everybody win. Cooperation is beginning to join competition as a business strategy. The secret is out: Someone does not have to lose in order for someone else to win.

With the advent of burgeoning cooperation, the Harvard Business School wizards must be wondering about the appropriateness of one of their latest seminars. It's very competitively entitled "Hardball Strategy: Are you Playing to Play or Playing to Win?" The accompanying promotional copy seems unusually combative. "It's a fact of life," it hectors, "—on the harsh playing field of business, nice guys finish last, and ruthless competitors take all."

Yet what it takes to be a successful competitor today is distinctly different from what it took only a few years ago. The focus of corporate strategy has shifted from dominating markets and besting competitors to building alliances.

Call it "cooperating to compete."

Consider the airlines. The key to success—or at least survival—in this tough industry today is code sharing, a process that enables airlines to market flights jointly. Continental, for example, books a flight on Air France, in effect increasing its route system. But there's more than just marketing and revenue enhancement going on here. The "Sky Team" alliance, which enables the two airlines to cooperate rather than compete, has also enabled both airlines to reduce their costs by joining forces in purchasing fuel, typically one of an airline's largest expense items. The partnership also reduces administrative expenses, like ticketing and sales functions. It's even a win-win for air travelers, who can now move seamlessly among different carriers and have additional route and fare choices, as well as new opportunities to accrue frequent flyer miles.[14]

In the health care industry, hospitals are joining together to cut costs by sharing everything from high-tech equipment to laundry service. In education, not-for-profit colleges and universities are collaborating with one another to strengthen their positions in the education marketplace. They're also building alliances with for-profit enterprises. Washington University, for example, has forged an unlikely joint research agreement with chemical giant Monsanto with the following quid pro quo: The university gets access to $26 million for research, and Monsanto gets access to the patents that result. In pharmaceuticals, a technology-sharing alliance between Eli Lilly and Denmark's Novo Company has produced a new insulin product that has leapfrogged Squibb's efforts.

Cooperators, rather than *competitors*, are on the ascendant. These temporal intelligence innovators see the marketplace not as a "we/they" world, but as a continuing commercial community full of new concepts and—you guessed it—even newer jargon. This presumably kinder and gentler economy is called, for example, "co-opetition." In it, customers, suppliers, and competitors become part of a "value net," as do "complementors" (other businesses that add value to a product or service, like Intel chips for Microsoft's latest software).

Business, it turns out, does *not* have to be war.

But it can get pretty contentious. Ocean Spray, the giant cranberry coop, recently decided to compete rather than to cooperate. Having turned down an alliance with Pepsi that many saw as hugely beneficial, its board of directors ordered management to stay independent and turn Ocean Spray into a "business to be reckoned with." Yet the ensuing competitive battle could decimate Ocean Spray. As Tom Pirko, who heads a beverage industry consulting firm, told a reporter, "The equation just doesn't work. It's a matter of economics, capabilities, and resources. The numbers all lead to one conclusion: Ocean Spray can't do it on its own."

There is, however, a ray of hope. Ocean Spray CEO Randy Papadellis, who showed his managerial acumen when he shaved millions off expenses by reducing the thickness of corrugated shipping containers, is beginning to explore win-win partnerships with other major beverage companies. He has cut a cooperative deal with the beer and beverage company Sapporo in Japan and with Gerber Foods in the United Kingdom. As long as they don't demand equity, Papadellis is willing to talk. By creating alliances rather than enemies, he says, "We can tap into the scale other companies have."[15]

▋ INFINITE GAMES

We were delighted to discover how nicely theologian and writer James Carse's thinking resonated with our time masters' sense of applied continuity. In his book *Finite and Infinite Games*, Carse conceives of life (and, we would add, managing and leading) as being made up of *two* kinds of games. There are *finite* games, those that have precise beginnings and are played with a rigid set of rules. They end only when someone—a person or a team—wins or when time runs out. These are the familiar and time-managed contests of daily life, the games we play when we develop competitive strategies.

Then there are *infinite* games. These are more complex and harder to understand, but ultimately more pleasing, more profitable, and less competitive. Infinite games are played with rules that change whenever the game is threatened with a finite outcome—i.e., the possibility that someone might win and someone else lose. The objective is to bring as many people into the game as possible, and to continue the game. The secret, claims Carse, is to keep finite games in infinite play, and to continuously change them.[16]

That Möbius strip that we mentioned earlier is, appropriately enough, widely used to represent the "shape" of Carse's endless gaming. But, like co-opetition, it reminds time masters that improving play may be more important than winning, that the victors teach the vanquished rather than obliterate them, and that it is generally better to develop new markets than to fight over old ones.

Shona Brown and Kathleen Eisenhardt's research on organizational change supports this idea. Their study of Microsoft suggests that continuity is a fundamental part of the software giant's corporate strategy. They noted that Microsoft's remarkable trajectory since its inception has consisted not of dramatic spikes and brilliant tactics, but instead of a continuous series of moves, made over the years, that have combined into a supremely successful business model. It's a strategy process that "does not look much like 'do an industry analysis, pick a strategic position, and execute.' It does not really resemble 'examine our core competencies and build off of them.' It looks a lot more like a 'creation of a relentless flow of competitive advantages.'"[17]

That relentless flow explains many business success stories, including the famous and hugely successful start-up of office supplies giant Staples. From a single store in Brighton, Massachusetts, founder Tom Stemberg built what today is an $11 billion company with nearly 1,500 retail outlets and thereby revolutionized the way we buy everything from ballpoint pens to desk chairs. The company's growth was evolutionary. As Stemberg once put it, "For me there was no

'Eureka' moment with Staples—it was a confluence of moments."[18]

Brown, Eisenhardt, and Stemberg are not the only panjandrums of corporate strategy who have caught on to the importance of continuity. Many strategic consultants, having for too long ignored the temporal aspects of strategic choice, have begun to define their field as a *flow* or *stream* of organizational actions, one that helps to examine, for example, how quickly a firm should diversify, what organizational forms it might adopt over time, and just when the benefits of diversification might appear. Such dynamic strategic thinking challenges the conventional wisdom that time consists of discrete units of measurable and equal duration (think "clock time") and opens up the remarkable possibility that time—particularly when it comes to strategic planning—can best be thought of as a continuous before/after series of events.

■ THE PERILS OF MONOCHRONICITY

The heroes of flow and continuity are those multitasking *polychrons* we referred to above. (You probably *are* one if you are extraverted, find change exhilarating, tolerate ambiguity well, are formally educated, strive to achieve, are impatient, and—no surprise—are late more than you'd like to admit.) Rather than plowing through a meticulous daily to-do list, they comfortably tolerate, and frequently even encourage, interruptions and changes in their daily plan.

This temporal improvisation turns out to be amazingly productive. Polychrons, in fact, report that going with, rather than fighting against, the maddening flow actually helps them achieve their daily goals. Meanwhile, their monochronic compatriots, dutifully slogging their way though one activity at a time, frequently come up short.

This should come as no surprise. It is increasingly impossible to forecast and organize each day because there are so many unpredictable disruptions. Worse yet, attempting to impose a sense of order on this chaos by assigning priorities to each and every task often makes matters worse. Such an obsessive urge to organize often blocks the spontaneity required for success in a tumultuous environment. Effective leadership is frequently a very impromptu performance. As Bluedorn puts it, "Managerial work is polychronic work."[19]

Do the arithmetic. While monochrons diligently protect their temporal turf, polychrons create temporal synergies that yield a lot more bang for the buck. It's the difference between the cooks one of us came to know while serving in the Navy and the chefs one discovers in a fine restaurant.

Onboard a U.S. Navy frigate, one of us discovered in a previous life, there is the kind of monotonously sequenced order that one expects to find in the military. This methodical approach to things permeates the entire ship, even the galley. If, for example, a dinner menu calls for roast beef, green beans, and potatoes, the cooks, having come on duty at 4 a.m., first roast the beef, then boil the potatoes, and finally cook the beans. The unavoidable consequence of this lockstep monochronicity is a kind of culinary mediocrity generally reserved for steam tables and third-rate buffets—tough, overcooked meat, tasteless mashed potatoes, and undercooked string beans. Compare this with a good chef's polychronic and very simultaneous juggling of everything: plating desserts, finishing off a bacon-wrapped dove breast, and firing the vegetable purveyor.

Not too long ago, polychronicity was thought to be

evidence of a helter-skelter mentality, workplace attention deficit disorder, poor time management, or downright reck-lessness. Sometimes these charges are true, of course. (Consider, for example, the well-documented risk of driving while operating a cell phone.) But research has lately shown that leaders who can keep multiple balls in the air can far exceed the output of those who put in twenty-four hours of monochronic activity.[20]

What's more, it's healthy. Polychronic social behavior—lots of friends, lots of activities, vibrant social networks, whether at the office or at home—is a powerful antidote for depression and malaise. Continuous involvement in social networks leads to enhanced health outcomes: fewer colds, less depression, lower rates of heart disease and cancer. A dramatic rule of thumb, constructed by Robert D. Putnam, whose breakthrough book *Bowling Alone* assesses the growing disconnectedness in modern American society, is this: "If you belong to no groups but decide to join one, you cut your risk of dying over the next year in half."[21] To be continuously connected matters to our lives in the most fundamental way. Disengagement means discontinuity.

Gestalt therapists (we turned to them when we discovered that the German word *gestalten* meant "organized wholes") would agree. They know that we all have emotional blocks within us—the urgency of insistent daily schedules and clock obsession come to mind. The goal of Gestalt therapy is to dissolve such barriers by getting patients to focus on *process*—what is being done, thought, and felt at the moment—rather than on what was, might be, could be, or should be done.

The idea is that unfettered emotions are, in fact, terribly important. They are the guides and continuous controllers of our every behavior. Anything *but* a hindrance to rational thought and behavior, emotions constitute the streaming media of our awareness and spontaneity. A marvelous feedback device, they ceaselessly report on the environment around us, identifying risks and hazards, opportunities and possibilities. They herald continuity. We just need to listen.

■ CHOOSE YOUR SPORT

We are not surprised that, during discussions of continuity, time masters invariably talk about sports. A football team, long an exemplar of business management, seems in many ways to mirror a highly efficient factory. There's the scheduling and sequencing of a complex set of activities. The football, like an automobile on a production line, moves constantly toward its goal during a scoring drive. And there's a gaggle of specialized departments and hierarchies: offense, defense, special teams. Yet football, when looked at from a temporal standpoint, is anything but continuous. It is a series of violent actions interspersed with periods of inactivity. "The game," as sportswriter David Harris once put it, "proceeds in short bursts of synchronized combat broken by pauses to regroup."[22] It is won one play at a time.

Then there is baseball, surely a game that mirrors the world of work, albeit in very different ways. Baseball celebrates the possibility that each player can transcend the organization. It is a sport dominated by individualistic, freewheeling, charismatic mavericks. The game pauses when teams leave and take the field between innings. Players come to bat one after another. And, even though baseball is one of the few team sports with no conventional game clock, baseball time is clearly tolled by the discrete tops and bottoms of innings.

Interestingly, though, basketball is the sport that most thoroughly fascinates our time masters. They tend to see in the game an almost perfect example of applied continuity and flow. There is constant movement up and down the court, near-instantaneous reaction to other players and their moves, and riveting spontaneity. As one basketball devotee put it, "Go to a pro football game and it looks choreographed. Go to a baseball game and it looks like croquet. But go to a pro basketball game and it looks like anything could happen at any second—and it usually does."

Organizational development expert Dick Daniels, whose passion is building championship organizations, says that the appeal of basketball is the way the game flows. Successful teams play a game that can be described only as marvelously fluid and adaptive. There's a rhythm that you can see in the repetitive bouncing of the ball, the flow of play on the court. "In basketball," writes Daniels, "offense and defense flow together. One of the most exciting moments in a football game is when a turnover occurs—perhaps three to four times during the course of the game. In basketball, this transition situation happens about three or four times every minute."[23]

And in basketball these changeovers between offense and defense are uninterrupted, a part of the flow. Unlike football (with its interminable time-outs) and baseball (with its interruptions between batters and innings), a fast-breaking basketball game resembles nothing so much as an unstoppable rushing river. The coach does not insist on specific plays, but choreographs the speed and direction of this flow. After all, as Robert Keidel, sports enthusiast and former Senior Fellow at the Wharton Applied Research Center, puts it, "A basketball game is a flow of plays that cannot be 'programmed' in advance like a football game or a baseball game. Even the scoring, and the excitement, is continuous." No wonder basketball fans spend more time standing than they do sitting![24]

The payoff of seeing time as continuous is anything but trivial. It enables strategically oriented time masters to envision their business and organization in the future, interpolate their way backward into the present reality, and then manage their implementation more powerfully. One-time Citicorp strategy guru Stanley Davis saw this as a provocative riddle, best solved with a clear mind. "The present is the past of the future," he said, "and [time masters] can *push* the strategy toward its realization rather than be *pulled* along by it."[25]

We have all been guilty of being driven by clocks and calendars—in fact, we often depend on them. It's useful to know that the nine o'clock meeting will end promptly at ten and that the car will pick us up fifteen minutes later so that we can catch our noon flight. Clocks and calendars are necessary for an orderly society, not to mention a modicum of sanity. But it is important to ensure that a continuous common thread runs through this very staccato chaos.

Time masters provide members of high-performing teams with conditions that facilitate the sense of flow. They ensure that individuals' skills meet the challenge, that team members feel connected with one another, and that distractions are minimized. As a result, team members become so immersed in achieving a goal that they frequently lose track of time. For people in the flow, the task becomes a source of peak experience. Time masters' temporal intelligence enables them to trigger flow by presenting followers with significant challenges that demand both freedom and creativity.

Time masters facilitate and celebrate the subtle (and

sometimes not so subtle) outcomes that flow brings in order to make others aware of it. They ensure that the raw ingredients for continuity and flow are designed into the work of everyone on their team. Most importantly, they always seek to balance the challenges they make with the skill levels of their colleagues, always stretching both a bit, just to raise the bar.

Let the games begin . . . and continue.

■ HOW YOU CAN APPLY TEMPORAL INTELLIGENCE

You depend on clocks and calendars. But remember that minutes and hours are not natural phenomena; give them only the importance they deserve. Sometimes *flow* requires a more sophisticated view of time. Here are some things you can do to convert discontinuity into continuity:

■ Transform the finite game of business—the assumption that there must be winners and losers—into an infinite game. Stop worrying only about winning, and start thinking about improving the game. An example: Quit competing for mature markets and begin growing new ones.

■ Stop trying to do everything; it's not your job. Your job is to continuously achieve goals and objectives through the efforts of others. Cross several things off your to-do list. You will probably find that the sun still rises—and chances are that your business does, too. Discover the joy of doing fewer things better.

- Don't close meetings—leave them open. It keeps people thinking. Ten minutes of meeting can buy you ten *days* of thinking. The resulting hallway double-takes mean that your team is processing the problem and beginning to own it. A movable feast, a party on the move.

- Create organizational continuity by staying on message. Time masters provide a strong and un-wavering voice of leadership via speeches, memos, e-mails, board meetings, or interactions in the hallway. Their consistent message echoes throughout the organization. They sustain enthusi-asm, not in flashy spikes and bursts, but day in and day out.

- Create flow. Time masters provide members of high-performing teams with the conditions that fa-cilitate the sense of flow. They match challenge with capability. They ensure not only that individ-uals' skills meet the challenge, but that those indi-viduals feel connected with one another, and that distractions are minimized.

- Don't allow routine calendar line items to take pre-cedence over the really important issues. Time masters constantly evaluate how that next block of time should be invested—deciding, for example, to continue with an impromptu but productive conversation in the hall even if it means rearrang-ing the rest of the day. They treat their calendar-ized time as suggestive rather than definitive, a work in progress.

CHAPTER 3

TIME'S AMAZING ELASTICITY

TRY AN EXPERIMENT.

It involves an old-fashioned sandglass, now known as an hourglass or three-minute egg timer. Fill one end with sand, then turn it over and watch the sand pass from the upper chamber to the lower.

Everyone knows intuitively that the sand must flow through the bottleneck at a constant rate. Yet the sandglass presents us with an apparent paradox. When the upper chamber is full, it seems that the amount of sand in it decreases at a slow, steady rate. But when it is about half empty, we perceive that the speed of the emptying sand increases.

And then, when it is almost empty, the flow seems to increase exponentially. Now time, which seemed so languid before, races ahead. This is not only a metaphor for how events seem to flash by as we grow older, but also an example of the variability in how we perceive time.

One of us recently noticed this disarming Alice in Wonderland effect while making a presentation to a large audience of executives. The host had emphasized that it was important to end the presentation precisely at noon, so that the participants could proceed to lunch. A small clock was installed on the podium. There were seven major points to cover, each embellished with short film clips and the inevitable PowerPoint slides. Time moved surprisingly slowly as the first four topics were covered; the hands on the clock seemed barely to move. But as the fifth point was covered, the clock seemed to speed up, going faster and faster. In the middle of the sixth point the clock suddenly read five minutes before noon. The final five minutes raced by as if they were seconds. Not surprisingly, the presentation ended abruptly, with no time to cover the final point.

Time, it seemed, had melted away.

This experience called to mind a provocative image of time's elasticity, created one summer evening after a party on the Costa Brava. Salvador Dali was preparing to paint one of his favorite scenes—the rocks and barren olive tree fronting the tiny bay near his home. As Dali studied the familiar landscape, he suddenly remembered a plate of soft Camembert cheese that had been served with dinner. It gave him an idea, a way to make *this* landscape different from all the rest.

The result is history's best-known surrealist painting, *The Persistence of Memory* (Figure 3-1). Its odd forms and juxta-

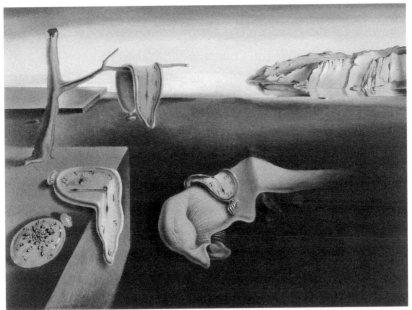

Figure 3-1. The Persistence of Memory. *(© 2004 Salvador Dali, Gala-Salvador Dali Foundation/Artists Rights Society (ARS), New York).*

positions make it unforgettable. In the infinite distance, the cliffs of Cap de Creus shimmer in the quiet water. In the foreground, an open pocket watch sits like a saddle on the neck of a misshapen head. Another swings in the breeze, a piece of laundry on a branch of the olive tree. A third seems to be "melting" over the edge of a rectangular cement block.

This "Camembert of time and space," as Dali called his masterpiece, is as relevant today as it was in 1931 when he painted it. His surrealistic image reminds us of the ubiquity of time. Our clocks and their insistently precise bulletins are everywhere: on our wrists, next to our beds, and in our radios, television sets, and cell phones. More than that, Dali's watches, as soft as overripe cheese, challenge the concept of exact, mechanical time in our lives and in our organizations.

Time begins to lose its conventional meaning. The watches (some have said that they represent the past, the present, and the future) dissolve and soften and become fluid.

Dali's extraordinary image helps us to see time as not just objective, but also subjective. Those melting watches, and the elastic time they represent, are in the process of transforming, like all human creations. Dali's most famous painting expresses a reality about time that is beyond the conventional wisdom; it transcends time, suggesting that time can vary greatly in human perception.

Dali was right. Time, it turns out, is anything *but* regular, even though most of us have spent our lives taking its metronomically insistent ticks and tocks for granted. Increasingly, it is time's *irregularity* and astonishing malleability that is fascinating scholars and laypersons alike.

◼ SEEING WITH A SAILOR'S EYE

Pretend for a moment that you're speeding up Route 1 in California, the renowned two-laner that winds its way along the Pacific coast. The views of the ocean are spectacular, but the highway is notorious for being one of California's most dangerous roads. Coming out of a blind curve, you decide to pass the car ahead. As you drift into the oncoming lane, you see a car speeding toward you. No problem. You jam the accelerator to the floor.

It seems simple.

Yet navigating successfully around other cars depends on the solution to a rather complex problem, one that requires a fundamental reframing of the concepts of time, motion, and place. After all, we usually reckon time, motion, and place with respect to something fixed, like the next town, the driveway of our home, our car's speedometer, a clock, or even the North Star. This idea is based on common sense: Only if you know where you are (navigators call this a "fix") can you get to where you want to go. However, knowledge of absolute location, as important as it is to navigating from point A to point B, is woefully inadequate if, like those cars, both points are moving. Under these considerably more complicated conditions, things become fluid, in motion, malleable.

In this universe, nothing is absolute. Ever since Albert Einstein proposed his *special theory of relativity* in 1905, we have known that time itself is a *relative* construct, different for objects (or people) traveling at different speeds. Everything is relative.

So as you accelerate to pass the car ahead and dodge the one speeding toward you, you simplify matters by focusing on just one thing: the movement of the other cars with respect to your own car. This requires the ability to switch from an *absolute* spatial-temporal framework ("How many more minutes to Carmel?") to a *relative* framework ("Is that car that I am passing drifting backward with respect to my car?").

To do this, you must do something that seems very odd. You must imagine yourself as stationary, putting yourself into a temporal vacuum, even though you are hurtling along at seventy miles per hour. This capacity to place yourself, at least for a critical few moments, at the center of a frame of reference is called "a sailor's eye." It has prevented many collisions at sea and on the road.

Reframing time from absolute to relative has enabled two researchers to look at organizational strategy in a new light. Professors Arkalgud Ramprasad of Southern Illinois University and Major Wayne Stone of the Air Force Institute of Technology call it "strategic time."[1]

They describe this sense of time using the metaphor of a ship's radar, the navigational device that enables sailors to "see" other ships and land masses no matter what the weather conditions or time of day may be. On the round scope, a radial cursor extends from the center and traces echoes on each sweep around the screen. With each rotation, other ships change their position slightly on the fluorescent screen, their pips forming tracks.

There is, however, no track for the transmitting vessel. Like your car, it remains stationary in the middle of the display, while each target's track shows the relative motion between it and the transmitting ship. The radar scope, in other words, shows *succession* (the sequence of events) and *duration* (the interval separating events). Time relates one motion to another. A radar scope is, in essence, a strategic timepiece.[2]

Instead of a ship, place your organization at the center of the scope. Its constantly moving "targets" are its multiple constituencies: competitors, governments, employees, stockholders, consumers, and suppliers, each of which must be carefully tracked. Each sweep of the cursor reveals their relative motion. A new product is launched. An alliance is formed. A hostile takeover is in the offing. New regulations are passed. A senior executive is fired.

Patterns begin to form. The dots start to look like intelligence instead of raw data. Meaning emerges. Each pair of radar pips and their tracks provides a basis for measuring time. And the relationships between the tracks become an entirely new kind of clock, one that measures not absolute time, but time in the strategic—and very relative—universe. What strategists (let's call them *organizational navigators*) are looking for are strategic events: two competitors launching new products at the same time, for example. An alliance being crafted between major industry players. New technologies.

Time masters, having learned not to rely solely on clock or calendar time, want to "see" temporal maps akin to the perceptual maps that simplify confusing competitive landscapes by revealing changes in the marketplace. Like navigators who glean critical information from dots on a radar screen, they know that the right time to act is almost always determined by the competition and the market, not by the clock. No wonder they are likely to ask, "How fast is the competition going, and in what direction are they heading?" rather than, "Will they launch their new product in the third quarter?"

The sea, it seems, is the focus of many stories about time's elasticity. In her remarkable book *The Hungry Ocean*, for example, swordfish boat captain Linda Greenlaw describes what she calls "sea time":

> While steaming, the passage of time is measured in distance rather than hours, miles being more powerful than so many sweeps of the second hand. And with the exception of standing watches, the crew and myself are seldom aware of the time of day. An experienced crew member never asks "When will we be there?" but instead might inquire "How many more miles?" At sea, I am almost never cognizant of what day of the week it is, but am keenly aware of how many days must pass to bring the next full moon, the concept of time twisting to meet what is meaningful.
>
> Once we reach the fishing grounds, and the first set is made, the measure against which to mark the passage of time shifts from distance to the number of sets made and

pounds of fish onboard. Fishing days are not marked with a conventional clock; eight p.m. has no significance. Dusk is the time to start setting out, and daylight is the time to begin hauling back. Anything between dusk and dawn can be described by the number of sections of gear in or out, whichever applies. Crew members rarely, if ever, wear wristwatches.[3]

Put simply, the important thing is not clock time, which we've become so used to thanks to the linear models of time management, but *strategic* time—the ways in which each event connects with other events.

The lesson in this is that we sometimes need to take a very different perspective on time from what conventional wisdom would suggest. Time mastery requires that we put clock time in its place. It is a starting point, to which we must add knowledge of the events and tracks swirling around us. Like basketball players whose "court sense" gives them a perceptual capability that translates into points, time masters know that they must not be clock-watchers, lest the competition pass them by.

■ THE LOST TEN MINUTES

Think once again about driving—this time all the way back to when you first learned to drive.

Driving a standard shift vehicle, in particular, is daunting at first. You need to think about every detail in sequence: Push in the clutch; shift into first gear; release the clutch at precisely the right moment while feathering the gas pedal; accelerate until the sound of the engine tells you to repeat the process and shift again. Then there is proper braking to worry about, and learning to use your mirrors, and maintaining a constant speed—to say nothing of merging onto freeways, three-point turns, and parallel parking. At this stage, driving is a complex task, and not at all routine.

Soon, though, you don't have to think nearly so much about shifting or braking or merging. The task of driving is still just as complex as it was before, but it becomes increasingly routine for you. Eventually, you reach a stage where most of the time you don't consciously think about driving at all. Driving becomes so routine for us that we defamiliarize ourselves with its component tasks. Have you ever been driving to work along the route you take every day, when suddenly you arrive at a certain stop sign and realize that you can't remember getting there? That you can't remember anything specific for the past ten minutes? If so, then you have become defamiliarized with driving. The complex task of driving has become routine for you, automatic.

This experience can be somewhat jarring. You wonder, what if a dog had run in front of you during those ten minutes? Would you have even seen it? Exactly how close to oblivion were you during this apparent blackout? In truth, you (and the dog) were probably not in any real danger. It wasn't that you blacked out; it was just that driving now requires little of your conscious mind's attention. You were on autopilot. In the zone. Had a dog run into the road, you would no doubt have reacted appropriately.

Something fascinating is happening here, and it has to do with your perception of time. Objectively, you know that the ten minutes didn't go anywhere. Yet you can't remember them. It was like a dreamless sleep, one of those times when you doze off and feel that you woke up "instantly," when in fact it was hours later. Yet these lost ten minutes were very different from sleep. You were not only awake but productive during those minutes—in fact, you were carrying out a complex task.

Research into the psychology of time perception offers some insight into our lost ten minutes. It seems that defamiliarization (also known as *routine complexity*) is a recognized cause of this strange time-compressing effect. If a routine task is too simple, then boredom results and time seems to pass slowly. If a task is *complex* but *not routine*, then it requires our conscious attention and time seems to pass slowly. But when a task is complex enough to sufficiently engage the brain, yet familiar enough to be routine, then time shows its elasticity quite clearly—it actually seems to flow at a faster rate.

For example, consider the job of dispatcher for a natural gas company—the person who routes the firm's gas though various pipelines and allocates it to customers. On gas pipelines, most business must be scheduled in the morning in order to accommodate network planning. This means there is an intense period of activity each morning: watching multiple computer monitors; paying attention to the gas futures market; making multiple phone calls to suppliers, pipelines, and customers. The tasks are often quite complex, yet they are routine for experienced dispatchers, who nearly always describe mornings as "flying by."

The implication of this effect is to strive for routine complexity in certain situations. For naturally repetitive jobs, design the work flow so that employees' brains are appropriately engaged, but don't necessarily lose the routine. Presenting employees with new or unusual problems may seem like job enrichment, but it may also have the effect of slowing time for them. Obviously, the best course of action will depend on the process and the people involved; experimentation and adjustment will be needed. Routine complexity doesn't guarantee that time will pass more quickly (after all, driving doesn't *always* speed up time), but under the right conditions, you can affect time perception.

Some jobs, on the other hand, are actually monotonous and slow-moving because of the *absence* of time pressure. If all you're familiar with is the assembly-line environment, this may be difficult to believe. But ask an office worker how urgent that project on his desk is, and you may be surprised—and dismayed—by the answer. Not only is this bad for the company, for obvious reasons, but it makes time drag for the employee. Even a seemingly inconsequential job—labeling file folders, for example—can become challenging and rewarding when speed is a real issue. Time pressure, in other words, can sometimes *increase* job satisfaction. It all depends.

Jonathan L. Freedman and Donald R. Edwards, psychologists at the University of Toronto, have contrasted the game of chess with popular computer games to make the point. Although expert chess players may place time limits on moves, many people derive great pleasure from the game without imposing any time limitation. The reason, of course, is that even with all the time in the world, there are still no "perfect" chess games. Contrast this with a typical computer game. Without time limits on each move or a competing racer in the next car, even the most exciting game quickly becomes boring.

From an employee's standpoint, time pressure can sometimes become a proxy for the value of the task at hand. And it can, if managed properly, help make time fly.

■ EINSTEIN'S PRETTY GIRL AND THE DEPARTMENT OF MOTOR VEHICLES

"When a man sits with a pretty girl for an hour, it seems like a minute," Einstein observed. "But let him sit on a hot stove for a minute and it's longer than any hour."

Ask one hundred people to describe moments when time seemed to pass particularly slowly for them, and chances are that ninety-nine will mention time spent waiting in line somewhere: at the bank or the airport or the Department of Motor Vehicles. They may chuckle when they say it, but there is actually something to this notion. Management science has long recognized time's elasticity and the significant difference between *actual* and *perceived* time spent waiting in queues. When you're stuck in line, time does seem to pass more slowly.

The question, from a time mastery standpoint, is whether organizations can *do* anything about this phenomenon. Two management scientists, Mark Davis and Janelle Heineke, reviewed the extensive literature on queuing theory with an eye toward practical applications for service providers. Of the major factors that affect perceived waiting time, Davis and Heineke identified five that can be controlled by the firm.[4]

The first factor is the *perceived fairness* of the wait. Waiting lines are miniature societies, complete with their own unspoken rules and perceived injustices. Take a busy grocery store. Let's say that you are waiting in lane 3, with your cart full of Super Bowl snacks. Then a perky cashier announces that lane 4 is opening—but before you can maneuver your cart there, a man who was standing *behind* you in lane 3 beats you to the new lane, along with a number of other sprinters who you suspect haven't been waiting as long as you have. Quietly outraged by their audacity, you remain in lane 3. Regardless of your actual wait time, your *perceived* wait time will now be longer because of what you see as the unfairness of the situation.

Largely in response to this phenomenon, many service providers have switched to the "feeder" line, or the "cattle pen" system, popularized by Wells Fargo Bank during the 1960s. Here there are the usual multiple bank tellers (or cashiers, etc.) but just *one* long line guided by ropes or rails. When a teller position opens up, the next person in line is served. This ensures a low-anxiety, first-come-first-served approach with a high level of perceived fairness. Studies have shown that combined queues lead to shorter actual and perceived wait times, with some exceptions.[5]

The second controllable factor identified by Davis and Heineke is relatively obvious: the *comfort* of the wait. People who are uncomfortable nearly always perceive their waiting time to be longer than it actually is. Comfortable temperatures, places to sit or lean when practical, and aesthetically pleasing surroundings can significantly reduce perceived waiting time. Go to Disneyland, for example, and you may wait forty-five minutes for the new Indiana Jones ride—but the long queue snakes through a series of caves that look like old mining shafts and seem to be part of the ride. Who but Disney could transform a forty-five-minute wait into an entertainment experience? Restaurants, too, make waits more tolerable by inviting waiting patrons to relax in the lounge (thus turning waiting into a profit center).

The third controllable factor is the presence or absence of an *explanation* for the wait. Passengers waiting to board an aircraft tend to perceive a wait to be much longer than it actually is when they are offered no explanation for the delay.

But when they are told, "We need to de-ice the wings before boarding" or, "As soon as our first officer arrives from Dallas, we'll begin boarding," perceived wait time decreases. Perceived wait time increases, however, if customers see idle workers behind the counter. While this may not seem surprising, the magnitude of the reaction is: According to one study, such "observed idleness" is a more significant driver of perceived waiting time than is the inherent *importance* of time to the customer![6]

The fourth factor in perceived waiting time is whether the duration of the wait is *known or unknown.* To put it simply, a wait of known duration tends to seem shorter than an open-ended wait.

Consider these two scenarios. In scenario A, Julie goes to a restaurant and is told that the wait for a table is twenty minutes. Twenty minutes later, she gets a table. In scenario B, Julie places her name on a list for a table, but receives no estimated wait time. Twenty minutes later, she gets a table. In both cases, the actual waiting time is twenty minutes. But Julie's perceived waiting time in scenario B will tend to be longer, and it isn't difficult to see why.

In scenario A, after fifteen minutes have passed, Julie can say to herself, "Only five more minutes to go." In her mental accounting scheme, that doesn't sound like very long. Those last five minutes are relatively anxiety-free for her. She anticipates that she will soon get a table. It's the same effect that can make Fridays seem to fly by faster than Mondays—we know how close we are to the weekend. In scenario B, however, there is no such effect. In her nineteenth minute of waiting, Julie has no idea how much longer she has to wait, and this uncertainty tends to increase her perception of the wait's duration.[7]

Many restaurants exploit time's elasticity by *over*estimating waiting times in order to manipulate time perception. For instance, the restaurant may know that your table is likely to be available in twenty minutes. But the host will tell you to expect a thirty-minute wait. Assuming that you find that estimate acceptable and decide to stay, you will be pleasantly surprised if you are seated after just twenty-one minutes. Yet if you had been quoted a twenty-minute wait and it had taken twenty-one minutes, those twenty-one minutes would have seemed much longer. It's all about managing expectations.

Finally, customer perception can be affected by *initial versus subsequent waits*. A typical example is at the doctor's office. Often you will have to sit in the general waiting area with other patients before you are ushered into an examination room, where chances are that you will have to wait yet again for the doctor to arrive. Once more, perceived waiting time can be successfully manipulated. Patients sitting in the general waiting room tend to perceive time as passing very slowly, while those waiting in the exam room for the same amount of time tend to perceive time as passing relatively more quickly. This isn't to say that for most people, time spent in the exam room goes rapidly (it probably doesn't), but rather that patient perception of waiting time in the exam room is shorter.

The best thing to do, therefore, from a doctor's point of view, is to get patients into the system as soon as possible; patients feel that they are being better treated when they are waiting in the exam room, presumably because they perceive themselves to be closer to actual care—even if they aren't.

■ SIZE MATTERS: SPEEDING UP BY SCALING DOWN

During the 1970s, the University of Tennessee's Dr. Alton De Long designed an intriguing experiment.[8] Trained in both psychology and architecture, De Long ran a laboratory experiment that must have triggered the curiosity of faculty, students, and subjects alike. He created a number of environments, each a combination of an old-fashioned peep show and a dollhouse (complete with models of human inhabitants), and each differently scaled: one-twelfth of actual size, one-sixth of actual size, and so on. Subjects, all wearing special blinders that prevented them from seeing peripherally, were instructed to select one of the human figures in these ordinary household environments and then to imagine interacting with it. They were told to signal when they felt that thirty minutes had passed.

The experiment helped De Long further advance a hunch he had: that when it comes to time, *size matters*. Spatial scale (the size of an environment relative to the size of an observer), he believed, is a principal mediator in the experience of time and temporal duration. Subjects working in the one-sixth-scale setting, for example, reported that they'd done an hour's work when only twenty clock minutes had elapsed. And those who interacted with one of the even more Lilliputian figures in the one-twelfth-scale environment sensed that an hour of interaction had elapsed in only *ten* minutes of real time!

What this boils down to is that the perception of time can be influenced by the scale (or space) of the environment. In subsequent EEG studies, the experimenters showed that brain activity actually speeds up in proportion to scale—the smaller the scale, the faster the thinking!

De Long's experiments with miniaturized environments raise some very interesting questions. Is it possible to compress time by manipulating the scale of the problem? This is not science fiction. Just consider how contemporary adaptations of De Long's miniaturized models—they're called simulations—have sped up everything from product design to learning how to fly a Boeing 777 from New York to Paris.

Microsoft's "as-real-as-it-gets" Flight Simulator enables pilot wannabes to crawl into the minute cockpits of everything from single-seaters to 747s, contact air traffic control, roll down the runway, and fly from Charlotte-Douglas International to LAX in minutes. Another lets race car drivers like Aaron Povoledo, winner of the Canadian Formula Four Series, drive race tracks around the world before he risks crashing, spinning, and colliding on the real thing. In Maxis's wildly successful video game The Sims, you enter a bite-sized world where you control the lives of miniaturized avatars not unlike De Long's dollhouse inhabitants.

■ THE SIMS

It should come as no surprise that developers of management training have jumped onto this virtual bandwagon. There are a number of computerized simulations that attempt to recreate the business world in miniature.

One of our favorite simulations is Management Simulation Inc.'s Capstone, a complex Web-based simulation. Originally developed as an executive education program for corporate clients like General Electric, Motorola, and Honeywell, Capstone is now used at colleges and universities across the country, including Babson College, Penn State, Northwestern, the University of Michigan, and, we might add, our own Hartwick College.

Capstone mimics the electronic sensor industry—the supplier of the kind of gizmo that might be used in the manufacture of automobiles. Teams of four to seven participants assume the management of a fictional company. For eight hypothetical "years," teams make marketing, finance, human resources, manufacturing, and R&D decisions. After all the teams have entered their decisions, the facilitator clicks a series of buttons to process them. Within hours, or even minutes, teams see the results of their decisions in the form of detailed financial statements and market intelligence reports. This cycle continues as teams compete against each other year by year, adapting their strategies as they go.

MSI's web site (www.capsim.com) claims that Capstone "compresses time."

We agree. We have used management simulations for years, to great effect. At Hartwick College, our undergraduate management curriculum has been designed around computer simulations since 1996. Our Virtual Management Program combines classroom learning with a number of sims, each chosen for its coverage of a given learning objective. Our core financial management course, for instance, uses a finance-based sim called Fingame, our Global Business course one called the Business Strategy Game, our Marketing course one called Brands, and our introductory business course one called MikesBikes. The most powerful feature of these simulations is that students get to see results soon after making their decisions.

Simulations have their critics. For example, when we first proposed that our management curriculum revolve around sims, we encountered strong skepticism. How could a computer program mirror the rich, complex world of business? A simulation will be too simplistic, we were told. It will discourage creativity. Students will hate it. Besides, the algorithm on line 38,897 of the code is suboptimal.

Yet we are approaching the tenth year of the program, and our experience has been overwhelmingly positive. Even our most skeptical colleagues now recognize the immense value of well-designed and properly facilitated simulations. Yes, simulations do simplify real-world situations. Of course they have flaws and quirks. But our students consistently rate sims as the most valuable part of their management education at Hartwick. They enjoy the competition, the accountability, the team building—and, in particular, the quick payoff of seeing the results, good or bad, of their decisions. They often become completely absorbed in a sim, taking it as seriously as they might a real job. (It's not at all unusual to encounter team members in the hallway, passionately arguing over whether their "company" should issue equity or debt next quarter.)

Simulations harness the power of time's elasticity by compressing years of learning into a few weeks—not perfectly, perhaps, but better than anything else we have encountered. No student has ever come up to us and praised the "time-compression property" of sims in so many words, yet clearly that is what they value the most.

Why this rush to virtual reality? William Powell, who has studied the use of simulations in management development programs, puts it this way: "If the knowledge of how to react and interact isn't residing comfortably in your subconscious, then it's useless. That's what the best simulations promise to provide—something lifelike yet new and a chance to practice, practice, practice until the information or behavior becomes experience."[9] We would add to this the unique ability of simulations to speed up, or compress, time.

It's the kind of thing that the people at *Fast Company* magazine love. Open any issue and you'll find articles like

"Nineteen Ways to Take Charge Fast," "Fast Talk: Tough Sell," even a regular column entitled "Speedometer!" Clearly, this magazine's reason for being is to help its readers go faster. Not too long ago it celebrated Mobil Oil Corporation's Speedpass, the new payment-technology device that gets drivers in and out of gas stations as quickly as possible. The five million customers who now wave the tiny plastic gadget at the "flying horse" symbol on the gas pump shave about half a minute off what is normally a three-and-a-half-minute transaction. But more importantly, they average one more stop per month at Mobil stations than other customers, and they spend 2 to 3 percent more each visit.

Fast food will be next. Mobil is testing Speedpass in four hundred McDonald's outlets in Chicago. Next will come drugstores and grocery stores. Joe Giordano, the marketing whiz who dreamed up the Speedpass, seems to want to make everything happen faster. "Time," he told *Fast Company*. "That's the only thing I worry about at night."[10]

That may seem a bit obsessive. But perhaps losing sleep over time *is* appropriate. George Stalk, Jr., and Thomas M. Hout of the Boston Consulting Group have studied the relationship between quick response to customer needs and competitive position. By analyzing "time-based competitors"—firms like Wal-Mart, Citicorp, and Thomasville Furniture—Stalk and Hout concluded that going fast really counts. Wal-Mart replenishes its stock twice a week. Citicorp grants loan approvals in fifteen days. Thomasville "quick-ships" its furniture in an industry plagued by glacially slow deliveries. All three are reaching for a growth and profit advantage over their slower brethren.

These companies, and others like them, not only build and sell their products faster, but also significantly cut the time required to develop and introduce new products, reduce costs, offer broader product lines, cover more market segments, and rapidly increase the technological sophistication of their products and services. "The possibility of establishing a time-based advantage," write Stalk and Hout, "opens new avenues for constructing winning competitive strategies."[11]

■ SLOW TOWNS

Yet time mastery is not just about speeding things up. On occasion it's also about slowing time down, as we learned from Paolo Saturnini, mayor of the small Tuscan town of Greve-in-Chianti. Saturnini is the force behind a fascinating movement called *Città Lente,* or "Slow Cities," that is catching on in more than fifty Italian towns—places like Asti, Orvieto, and Positano. The movement got started when fast-food franchises began to pop up all over the Tuscan countryside. After the opening of one too many McDonalds, Saturnini and his compatriots became temporal revolutionaries, obsessed with slowing things down.

When Saturnini was interviewed in the fifteenth-century palazzo that houses the town hall, he delighted in telling a reporter of his town's prohibitions against the accoutrements of fast society: things like cell phones and their unsightly towers, fast-food chains, and car alarms. Saturnini doesn't want to sacrifice humanity for speed. "It's all about well-being for all of [Greve-in-Chianti's] inhabitants in terms of quality of life," he said. "Specialty and particularity are our wealth. They enrich our civilization, they enrich our time and they enrich our cities. We need to defend them."[12]

And that is what Saturnini and his sidekicks are doing. Like Marty and the nutty Dr. Brown in the classic time-travel film *Back to the Future*, the people of Greve-in-Chianti are going backward in order to go forward. To do this, they're combining their special brand of Italian Ludditism with the zeal of Chamber of Commerce boosters. They've discovered that slowing down is good business. After all, Tuscany's major industry is tourism. What could be more alluring to a time-harried visitor than a three-hour lunch in the town's main piazza?

Thomas Hylland Eriksen would agree. In his book *Tyranny of the Moment: Fast and Slow Time in the Information Age*, Eriksen bemoans the fact that the speed and tension of work has crowded out "slow time." As he puts it, we find ourselves with little, if any, time for the detailed, focused, and unhurried intellectual and interpersonal work upon which high performance depends. Time-saving technology has resulted in time's being scarcer than ever. "Slow time"—private periods when we are able to think and correspond coherently without interruption—is now one of the most precious resources we have, and it is becoming, according to Eriksen, a major political issue. Since we are now theoretically "online" twenty-four hours a day, he believes that we must fight for the right to be *unavailable*—the right to live and think more slowly.

Slowpokes like Saturnini and Eriksen have a noble heritage, going back to the ancient world. Fabius, a Roman consul in the third century B.C., had the unlucky job of being one of Rome's rulers when Hannibal crossed the Alps. The Romans, panicked by the threat of an imminent attack, demanded quick action. Yet Fabius had a different plan: Knowing that Hannibal's supply lines were stretched to their limit, he believed that delay, not fast action, was the right strategy. He would avoid risking his armies in pitched battles. He shadowed Hannibal closely as he headed south. Knowing that time was his ally and Hannibal's greatest enemy, Fabius turned that knowledge to his own advantage.

It worked. Unable to supply his forces adequately, Hannibal finally withdrew from Italy. It was slowness, not quick action, that saved Rome.

One of the most unusual examples of consciously slowing things down that we've encountered is going on in Halberstadt, an ancient town nestled in the Hartz Mountains of Germany. Here, a music theorist named Heinz-Klaus Metzger has become intrigued with a piece of organ music composed by John Cage, one of twentieth-century America's great musical innovators. Cage, who experimented with unusual percussion instruments, electronics, weird notation, and even silence, had composed a piece of music that he called "Organ2/ASLSP." The name itself seemed a curiosity, and when Metzger came to believe that "ASLSP" might mean "as slow as possible," he set himself on a mission to slow things down considerably in Halberstadt.

Encouraged by the availability of an old-fashioned mechanical organ equipped with a sustaining mechanism that allows notes to go on indefinitely, Metzger and a growing number of like-minded recruits were hooked. As he told two very curious reporters, "One could imagine playing the organ piece so slowly that it would take years to come to an end."[13] The result is an organ recital that began on September 5, 2001, and is expected to end in the year 2640.

It apparently came as no surprise that the house was empty on opening night, since Cage's score for "Organ2" begins with a musical silence that (using Metzger's time) lasted seventeen months. No matter. It provided time for the actual reconstruction of the organ. The opening three notes of "Organ2/ASLSP," making up a chord that could be heard twenty-four hours a day, were first played in February 2003, receiving rave reviews. Two more notes were added in July 2004.

A local businessman seems to appreciate Metzger's recital. Referring to Germany's economic troubles and corporate scandals, he told a reporter, "All these were done because of decisions that were made too quickly. My wish is that this project causes people to slow down and think out decisions more."[14]

A brief intermission is scheduled for 2319.

■ THE REVENGE OF THE TYPE Bs

People like Saturnini and Eriksen may seem hugely out of step in our go-fast world. Yet there is evidence that the type Bs may have it right.

The concept of aggressive, hard-charging type A personalities versus more sanguine type B individuals was originated by Meyer Friedman and Ray H. Resenmar in their book *Type A Behavior and Your Heart*. It probably comes as no surprise that Friedman and Resenmar found that type As tend to suffer from serious heart trouble more frequently; over the past thirty years, this fact has joined the realm of conventional wisdom. What *is* surprising is the single most defining characteristic of type A behavior, according to the men who coined the term. Type As are defined as having, above all, a "chronic sense of time urgency." Not aggressiveness, or a big ego, or unusually high aspirations, but time urgency.[15]

And things get worse for the time-obsessed type As. One study found that while aggressive type As represent as many as eight out of ten middle managers, they tend to disappear as you look up the corporate ladder.[16] Think of the CEOs you know, and this starts to sound more reasonable. There are certainly examples of successful type A executives (especially among self-made entrepreneurs), but in most organizations, the people at or near the top tend to seem a bit, well, calmer.

Slowing down can help companies as well as individuals. Consider a recent McKinsey & Company study of eighty Internet companies. The researchers sought to determine not only the speed with which each of them built its business, but also the outcome. Going fast, they discovered, gave an advantage to only 10 percent of the companies they studied. In high-tech start-ups, speed turned out to be a disadvantage because it gave the company less time to study the market, test its assumptions, and understand its competitors.

For all the glitz and glamour of the high-speed chase, so common in business nowadays, there are also many tortoise and hare stories—tales of firms that have learned, often at great cost, that slow and steady can win the race. Christine Chen at *Fortune* magazine calls it "the last-mover advantage." Thomas Eriksen senses these subtle dangers of our obsession with speed in his book *Tyranny of the Moment*. His biggest fear is that we are going so fast, and information is being delivered so rapidly, that we are forced to live "with our gaze firmly fixed on a point about two seconds into the future." Things change so quickly that new products seem outmoded by the time they are introduced. Speed becomes toxic and contagious, leading to a lesser eye for quality, to simplification, to a lack of attention and precision.

Not long ago, for example, according to *Fortune*'s Chen,

"Telecom giants were rushing to build networks everywhere they could." But Verizon waited on the sidelines—it was the industry's slow mover, and as a result it won the advantage because of an unforeseen fiber glut. Verizon was able to put together an international network out of segments purchased at bargain prices from telecommunications companies that were desperate to unload them.[17]

By going slow, Verizon saved over $300 million. The understated Tom Bartlett, president of Verizon's Global Solutions, Inc., summarized his company's brush with the last-mover advantage this way: "The timing worked out well for us."

■ WHEN TIME STOPS

You may have experienced time's elasticity yourself when an event seemed to pass much more slowly than usual. This can be explained. In his book *A Watched Pot: How We Experience Time*, Michael Flaherty describes a large-scale study of time perception. Flaherty examined hundreds of cases in which people claimed that time had "slowed down" for them—a phenomenon that he calls *protracted duration*.

Here are three first-person accounts cited by Flaherty:

- Armenians interviewed by *Izvestia* described in gripping simplicity the terror of the first moments of the quake. "It was like a slow-motion movie," said Ruzanna Grigoryan, who was working at the stocking factory in Leninakan, the republic's second-largest city, when the building began to tremble. "There was a concrete panel slowly falling down."[18]

■ At times, and with increasing frequency now, I experience a kind of clarity that I've never seen adequately described in a football story. Sometimes, for example, time seems to slow way down, in an uncanny way, as if everyone were moving in slow motion. It seems as if I have all the time in the world to watch the receivers run their patterns, and yet I know the defensive line is coming at me just as fast as ever.[19]

■ Once, whilst returning to school . . . I walked off [a raised walkway] and fell to the ground, but the height was only seven or eight feet. Nevertheless the number of thoughts which passed through my mind during this very short, but sudden and wholly unexpected fall, was astonishing.[20]

In all, Flaherty examined 705 such cases of protracted duration, trying to determine what causes the "slow motion" sense of time. Most cases, he found, were the result of negative events: suffering, intense emotion, violence, and danger, for example. Other factors that "fooled" the brain into thinking that time had slowed included boredom and intense concentration.[21]

■ SLOW-MOTION LEADERSHIP

The concept of slow-motion time is intrinsically interesting. But what could it possibly have to do with leadership?

Perhaps a great deal. There are times in any organization when things seem to spin out of control. The situation is chaotic. People lose direction. There is a flurry of activity, but little productivity. In times like these, a leader may wish for a way to slow time down—to stop the clock long enough to refocus the team and regain control.

Few of the causes of the slow-motion effect listed earlier would be desirable (or even possible) for a leader to emulate. You may be able to slow time by initiating violence or danger, as Flaherty found, but we don't recommend it. However, he identified one more, particularly intriguing cause of protracted duration: shock or novelty. Apparently many people feel that time slows down for them when, all of a sudden, something particularly unusual happens.

Time masters can use this technique to great effect.

A powerful example of temporal intelligence can be found in Steven Spielberg's film *Saving Private Ryan*, where Captain John Miller (portrayed by Tom Hanks) shows how a leader can stop time at a crucial moment. Miller's small band of soldiers is bickering over his recent decision to release a German prisoner of war. Voices are raised. One man is so upset that he threatens to leave. Tensions escalate. Guns are drawn.

Then Miller asks a question that is completely bizarre given the seriousness of the situation: "What's the pool on me up to right now?"

The question has nothing to do with the crisis, and Miller's men stare at him in disbelief. For weeks, they have been speculating about what Miller does for a living back home. They have even created a pool to bet on the correct answer. The pool has apparently reached about three hundred dollars.

The question stuns the men into silence. "I'm a schoolteacher," Miller announces flatly. "I teach English composition."

The unexpected change of subject catches the men completely off guard and reveals the absurdity of the conflict. Instantaneously, the tension dissipates. Miller quietly walks away, and one by one his men follow. Without raising his voice and without issuing any orders, Miller has taken command of the situation and averted potential disaster.

He has stopped time.

Such tactics are by no means limited to the movies. Simon Walker is the managing director of Challenge Business, a company that offers extreme leadership training events, such as crewing on a seventy-two-foot yacht from Boston to Southampton, England, or rowing—yes, *rowing!*—a thirty-six-foot boat across the same north Atlantic route. When things get hairy, as they frequently do, he hits "pause."

"During a crisis," he said in an interview, "my third command was always to put on the kettle. In the midst of chaos, no leader can deal with a crew of 18 upset people. By demanding cups of tea for the whole crew, I got one person out of my hair, and I introduced a normalizing factor into a crisis situation. If the skipper wants a cup of tea, it can't be that bad."[22]

He's right. Walker's ability to stop time reframes the problem, giving everyone the opportunity to think. By using novelty to manipulate time, he is—like Captain Miller—able to regain control of his crew.

▪ FASHIONABLY LATE

From the on-time performance of airlines to arriving at your theater seat before the curtain goes up, being on time is important: It is a behavior by which we measure character, assess reliability, and gauge another's efficiency and capacity to plan ahead.

No group better personifies punctuality than the Germans. World-class on-timers, they live in a country where operas begin precisely at 8:12 p.m. and buses arrive and depart as scheduled. An invitation for 4:00 p.m. means exactly that, 4:00 p.m. Traveling by train? You take your seat on the Inter-City Express running, say, between Stuttgart and Frankfurt. The schedule promises a 9:11 a.m. departure, and that is what you get. Always.

Just as the minute hand on the large platform clock clicks to eleven minutes after the hour, you feel a gentle tug, and you are on your way. Like clockwork. Even on the autobahn, all temporal contingencies are factored into the punctuality formula. As one Düsseldorfer told us, "I calculate to the minute how long it will take to reach a destination, adjust for weather and traffic conditions, the probability of mechanical trouble, and then add fifteen minutes just for the hell of it."

But then there's the very *un*-German behavior of tardiness, a predilection that is so much a part of human nature that it has become the stuff of legend. In Sophocles' *Antigone*, for example, Creon arrives too late to rescue his son and future daughter-in-law from their death chamber. More recently, General George Meade arrives late at Gettysburg, enabling the Confederate army to escape across the Potomac. Still more recently, Lewis Carroll's Alice falls into the topsy-turvy world of Wonderland chasing a rabbit who complains, "I'm late, I'm late, for a very important date."

Be tardy and suffer the penalties, goes the conventional wisdom. There are charges for late mortgage, gas, water, and electricity payments. Credit card companies collect $6.6 billion—about 7 percent of their revenue—in late fees. For a long time, Blockbuster Video turned late fees into a profit center. Until consumer lawsuits forced a change in policy, late fees were a whopping 15 percent of revenue.

Entire nations can be affected by tardiness. In Ecuador, where being late is estimated to cost more than $700 million a year, the federal government recently initiated a nationwide punctuality campaign. People are publicly berated for wasting other people's time. Stragglers are barred from entering meetings. Newspapers routinely print lists of public officials who are late to events. Lateness has become a matter of state policy, a behavior requiring monitoring and control.[23]

To show that it was serious, Ecuador's government held a major kickoff meeting for its punctuality campaign. The good news? The country's president showed up. The bad news? He was late.

Actually, tardiness has recently gained an unlikely cachet, thanks in part to gadgets like cell phones, pagers, messaging devices, and personal digital assistants. These ever-present clip-on devices almost always suggest that the wearer is savvy, plugged in, and in demand. High tech makes it easy, even cool, to be late—to stretch time.

Running behind schedule? Just punch in, call the voice-activated number, and announce your whereabouts and your estimated time of arrival. Suddenly you're no longer late: You're on your way, you're almost *there*. Appointments become moving targets. It's no longer about *you* arriving on time; it's about your *voice* arriving on time. Like other members of this new temporal class, you operate in what researchers call "soft time," a temporal zone in which everything is—you guessed it—relative.

High tech has melted time, and Dali would be delighted.

It has made tardiness, well, fashionable. As an article in the *Houston Chronicle* recently put it, "Expectations of where and when to meet shift constantly because people expect others to be constantly reachable. Eight-thirty is still 8 o'clock as long as your voice arrives on time—or even a few minutes after—to advise that you will not be wherever you are supposed to be at the appointed hour."[24]

We expect that time-stretching, unpunctual folks will increasingly challenge the conventional wisdom that life is about being on time. Perhaps Woody Allen was right: Eighty percent of success is showing up—even if it's just your voice that shows up.

■ HOW YOU CAN APPLY TEMPORAL INTELLIGENCE

Time masters know that time is, as Einstein discovered, elastic. They understand that clock time, although an important time *management* tool, contributes little to time *mastery.* Time masters would agree with William Faulkner, who wrote in *The Sound and the Fury*, "Time is dead as long as it is being checked off by little wheels; only when the clock stops does time come to life."

Here are some actions you can take to turn your knowledge of time's elasticity into practice:

- Stop crises by stopping time. Maintain your objectivity when a crisis occurs, rather than getting caught up in the subjective frenzy. Time masters "stop" time by asking *why* rather than *when*—or, better yet, by making a completely out-of-context suggestion, as Simon Walker does when he asks for tea in the midst of a storm at sea. Such reframing gives everyone an opportunity to reboot and brings fresh perspective to a problem.

- Don't restrict yourself to "clock time"—living by minutes and hours. As important as these can be, "event time"—the occurrence of meaningful events—can be even more important. Let events take precedence and trump the clock when necessary.

- Be aware of the time-related differences in team members. Recognize that everyone has a "time personality," a set of unique characteristics and individual differences that disposes each person to act and react temporally in different ways. Just as a team can benefit from a mix of personality types (à la Myers-Briggs), it can also function better if the team members have different senses of urgency, different time horizons.

- Slow time down. Recognize that top speed is not always the most appropriate pace. Take the time, if needed, to do more research or ask more questions. Don't get caught up in a momentum that might bring you to market before you're really prepared, or lead you to make a decision that isn't yet ripe.

CHAPTER 4

RHYTHM: THE BEAT
IS EVERYTHING

YOU'VE JUST ARRIVED at the site of your company's annual management development meeting. It's not the first time you've attended, and you have a sense of what's to come. As you unpack your bags and settle into your room, you begin to prepare for the first session, scheduled for 8:00 the next morning. When you open the thick binder containing your seminar materials, you are amazed to discover that the first half-day session is entitled "Art in Rhythm" and that it promises "to help you and your fellow participants understand the processes involved in building strong teams and in stimulating creativity."

Incredulous, you read on. "Every individual . . . has a

rhythm," the course description continues, "a customer has a rhythm, a client has a rhythm, a team has a rhythm, an organization has a rhythm, this whole world has a rhythm."[1]

Despite the hyperbole, you begin to get the picture.

After you arrive at the conference room the next morning, there is the familiar presentation, complete with slide show and handouts. The person sitting next to you yawns and says she is looking forward to dinner. Someone answers a cell phone. The coffee break provides a welcome opportunity to network. When you return, a trainer approaches the podium.

And then they bring out the drums.

There's something for everyone. Bongos. A big Brazilian surdo. A rattling kiwi fruit. Within minutes, you and your bewildered colleagues are equipped with an array of percussion instruments ranging from the strange to the familiar. An announcement is made: "Within fifteen minutes, everybody will be making beautiful music."

That prediction, it turns out, is overly optimistic. When everyone starts drumming, the noise is deafening. There is no discernible beat. Even so, you notice that several participants are beginning to sway back and forth. As the banging clumsily slows, the trainer proclaims, "This is the rhythm of organizational change." (There's nothing new about this. Anthropologists long ago discovered that drumming synchronizes even the most disparate groups into a shared rhythm.)

As the morning progresses, it becomes apparent that the trainer is right. A group rhythm begins to emerge from the chaos. Although it would not be confused with the percussion section of the New York Philharmonic, it's clear that the participants sense that rhythm goes beyond the toe-tapping cadence of a Dixieland rag or a Sousa march. It is a unifying force.

■ THE RHYTHM IS IN YOU

Anthropologist Edward T. Hall, in his remarkable book *The Dance of Life*, takes rhythm from music to motocross, where he discovers that one of the sport's superstars, champion desert racer Malcolm Smith, has it and uses it:

> It didn't seem to matter whether it was desert sand, arroyos and brush, mud, rocky mountain trails, or rough desert terrain. All the other riders were yanking on the handlebars, manhandling their machines around stones, logs, shrubbery, and bad ruts. Yet a film of Smith (*On Any Sunday*, with Steve McQueen) reveals a symphony of effortless ease. He would establish his rhythm at the beginning of the race and never deviate from it. Most remarkable was that this man who was passing everyone else did not seem to be going very fast. In fact, the other contestants, when looked at individually, actually gave the appearance of going faster than Smith. It was mind-boggling to watch a man traveling at such a leisurely pace consistently pass the furious speed demons.[2]

Hall calls this "effortless rhythm," the capacity to achieve timing so perfect that even the most complex activity looks easy. Time itself is captured by this rhythm. Its pace is slowed, its velocity made manageable. The Zen imperative that working too hard is the enemy of rhythm seems to be confirmed.

More dramatically, Hall used proxemics, a research method he pioneered that employs hidden cameras to record human movements. In one experiment, an associate filmed groups of children during recess on a school field. Afterwards, at the first viewing of the film, the researchers saw just what they expected to see—gaggles of children playing unremarkably in different areas of the schoolyard.

But then, when they ran the projector at different speeds, they noticed something quite stunning. One very active little girl stood out. She seemed to be everywhere, leaping, hopping, and twirling across the playground. To the researchers' amazement, each group of children she approached came into sync—not only with her, but with one another. Unwittingly, this whirling dervish was choreographing the entire playground. And she had brought the entire group to a kind of rhythmic consensus, a human synchrony. As Hall explains, "The music was *in them*. They brought it with them to the playground as a part of shared culture."[3]

Rhythm also plays a vital role in communication. Martin Luther King, Jr., and John F. Kennedy knew that a conversation's rhythmic properties give it meaning. At a more intimate level, listen to two people talking. You'll notice that each seems to be able to predict what's coming next in the stream of speech. Fascinating research done on conversation participants at the University of Pennsylvania has revealed that the syllables the participants stress fall into the same rhythm.

Jeremy Campbell, who plumbs the relationship between rhythm and conversation in his provocatively titled book *Winston Churchill's Afternoon Nap*, puts it this way: "When people meet and talk, they often behave more like musicians who improvise together with moment-to-moment precision. Such an encounter is both spontaneous and predictable at the same time."[4]

We've all got rhythm—it's one of the things that make us unique. Beat and cadence (in their musical and nonmusical forms) energize any occasion in which passion and enthusi-asm play a role. Rhythm is erotic and irrepressible, as researchers at the Montreal Neurological Institute recently discovered. Their scans of musicians' brains, made while their subjects listened to classics like Rachmaninoff's Piano Concerto No. 3 and Barber's *Adagio for Strings*, revealed neural activity similar to that triggered by food, sex, and addictive drugs.

Other studies—one of which suggests that singing in church produces endorphins that are known to promote social bonding—indicate that music is the "great communicator." It can help to strengthen social relationships and organize the activities of large groups of people.[5] While none of this persuades us that organizations could be made stronger by creating glee clubs, it may help to explain why we are regularly jarred out of our senses by over-the-top musical selections at business conferences and why, throughout the world, millions are spent on military bands. The right rhythm is an important survival tool.

Consider, for example, setting the tone of a critical meeting. To paraphrase Hall, you could—as in the opening passage of Beethoven's Fifth Symphony—start with a bang. That instantly recognizable Ta Ta Ta Taa announces with absolute clarity that this is *big*, it is *urgent*, it is *now*. If the boss starts the meeting by announcing, "Some-Thing-Is-Wrong," that's the dramatic equivalent of Beethoven's famous opening.

On the other hand, she might decide on a quieter opening, similar, say, to the diaphanous rhythms and tones of Debussy's *Clair de Lune*. This would enable her to slip into the conversation at just the right time.

Setting an effective rhythm can be tricky. Imagine the challenge of leading a symphony orchestra as it performs Ravel's *Bolero*, that famous melody that repeats itself eighteen times without change during the course of the piece. Renowned conductor Zubin Mehta reflected on *Bolero*'s very high potential for deteriorating into competing tempos and rhythmic divergence in the Oscar-winning documentary of the same name:

> There is a certain challenge which is in no other piece, really, because of the way *Bolero* builds up. *Bolero* starts from the first bar and continues. So keeping up the tempo, the pace, and not going forward in *Bolero* and not giving in to your instinct, which pushes you always, and to hold back, that's the tough part. I have seen performances or heard performances of *Bolero* where the side drum, for instance, in the middle of the piece is already at its peak. You can't do anything about it. Therefore, the conductor can't bring him down and build him up again. It's got to be done very, very carefully.

After watching a scene from this film, one time master, who resides in a small town in upstate New York, told a more down-to-earth story about divergent rhythms. After a winter storm, the young man he'd hired to shovel his driveway would arrive reliably at 5:00 a.m. to clear a path to the street. Just as reliably, the town's snow removal crews arrived between 6:00 a.m. and 6:30 a.m. Their huge plows cleared the street, he told us, opening the road but leaving his driveway impassable. Both the snow shoveler and the town snowplow had timetables that they scrupulously followed, yet the divergence of the two schedules worked only to the town's advantage. The street was clear, but it was frustratingly inaccessible to our blockaded homeowner.

Those two schedules set the rhythm of our colleague's

snow removal process. After a while, the two tempos, even though they conflicted with each other, created a recurring pattern of behavior.

This is called *entrainment*, the process by which different rhythms fall into synchronization with each other and then work in a parallel manner. In this case, however, it was only after our colleague suggested that the young man tune into the snowplow's radio frequency and adapt his schedule to the town's that these two divergent rhythmic patterns came into alignment.

■ THE POWER OF ENTRAINMENT

The concept of entrainment was described by a very observant seventeenth-century Dutch physicist named Christiaan Huygens. He was a remarkable man who had already invented the pendulum clock in an unsuccessful attempt to provide ships with the superaccurate timepiece needed to determine longitude. Ill and ordered to bed by his doctor, he noticed something very strange about two clocks that hung on his bedroom wall. They seemed to be communicating with each other, their pendulums oscillating together without variation. When stopped and restarted, the slower clock picked up its pace to become synchronized with the faster clock. To Huygens, the clocks' ability to alter their behavior was (to use his words) nothing short of miraculous.

So he experimented. He hung his clocks from iron hooks embedded in a beam, observing that when they were turned ninety degrees to each other or were separated by six feet or more, they ceased to tick and tock together. He then placed a makeshift wall between them. To his surprise, the clocks again ran in consonance, their pendulums swinging in opposite, but synchronous, directions. He hung each clock from a separate beam. Then he suspended them between two chairs, noting with surprise that when the pendulums were not in sync, the chairs began eerily to shake. Finally, when the pendulums once again achieved their reliable synchrony, the chairs were still and his bedroom was peaceful.

Unwittingly, Huygens had solved the problem of the "sympathetic" clocks. Like a falling row of dominoes standing on end, the clocks' swinging pendulums moved the boxes that encased them, which shook the planks, which wobbled the chairs.

But what do shaking chairs and ticking clocks have to do with leadership? We believe the process of entrainment not only applies to inanimate objects, as in the case of Huygens' synchronized clocks, but is also very human.

People possess a remarkable ability to sense, either consciously or unconsciously, the rhythms around them and to integrate those rhythms into their own. Entrainment is catching. Leaders with a high level of temporal intelligence are able to get people and teams to adjust their activity patterns so that they align closely with one another. They know that dissimilar rhythms cause most of the problems between individuals and between individuals and their environment. They know, too, that selecting the right rhythm can make or break organizational transformation.

João Vieira Da Cunha and his colleagues at MIT concur. As they put it, " 'When' [has been] added to the 'what,' 'how,' 'who,' and 'why' of change. Model organizations are those that are able to synchronize with the pace of those phenomena underlying their activity. . . . Managers, thus, play a very different role under this understanding of time. Their role is to foster the consideration of relevant rhythms."[6] This break-through idea does not mean that speed is unimportant. It means that incorporating "faster is better" with the right rhythm can provide an organization with an important competitive edge.

All this depends on temporal intelligence. To understand synchrony, mathematician Steven Strogatz suggests that we imagine several athletes running around a circular track. "Suppose these runners are friends, and they would prefer to run together so that they can talk," he says. He goes on:

> If their speeds are not too different—that is, if the slowest one can keep up with the fastest one, then you can get a group of runners all going in sync. But first, they have to be sensitive to each other. They have to be willing to adjust their speeds from what they would prefer. The fastest ones have to slow down, and the slowest ones have to speed up, to find some compromise. And that same principle— that slow oscillators have to speed up and fast ones have to slow down, and that this happens because of mutual inter-actions—is a pretty universal principle for synchrony.[7]

■ APPLYING ENTRAINMENT

Deborah Ancona and Chee-Leong Chong have moved en-trainment out of its traditional scientific context and trans-formed it into a leadership tool. Appropriately wary of the dangers of overstretching the analogy between the sciences and organizational behavior, they assert that successful en-trainment is fueled more by voluntary factors—such as intuition and human will—than by the rather deterministic factors seen in the pure sciences.

Ancona and Chong believe that when entrainment occurs, organizational performance improves. As they put it, "energy flows more effortlessly, and relations, performances, and feelings are enhanced."

Consider what happens when everyone on a team begins to operate at a pace that fits the situation. Ancona and Chong call this state *tempo* entrainment. R&D groups, for instance, entrain to the rate of technological innovation and scientific discovery. Marketing teams entrain to the pace of the market and its changing needs.[8]

Apparel manufacturer Zara exemplifies tempo entrainment. Its commitment to supply-chain discipline is revolutionizing the women's apparel industry. Ironically, this lightning-fast fashion house is based in northwest Spain's Galicia region, an area that has remained unchanged for centuries. Yet it has been revolutionizing the world of women's clothing.

In an industry known for its glacially slow market response (most of Zara's competitors ship only once a season), this trendy upstart has created "fashion on demand." It delivers twice a week from its mammoth warehouse to more than one thousand retail outlets in thirty-three countries, from Japan to Venezuela.[9]

Zara obsessively studies what everyone from TV stars to clubbers is wearing. It introduces thousands of newly designed women's jackets, skirts, and dress shirts each year, compared to the hundreds that competitors typically get to retail. It's no surprise that customers keep coming back to see what's new at this global marketing phenomenon. Or that Zara's CEO, José María Castellano Ríos, compares the shelf life of a new dress to that of a tub of yogurt. Zara has become entrained to the tempo of its customers, whose lives do not revolve around the arbitrary shows and business cycles of the fashion industry.

Tempo entrainment doesn't always mean moving fast. Sometimes, potential customers want things to slow down. Take one of life's biggest hassles, making a household move. Traditionally, of course, you—or the moving company's employees—spend a few frantic days sorting, wrapping, packing, tossing, and sleeping on hideaway beds. Then, on D-day, a giant truck and a team of loaders arrive, and within hours your former home is emptied of its contents.

Fortunately, there's a slower, gentler way. It's PODS, which stands for "personal on demand storage." PODS is another company that—like Zara—is marvelously entrained to its customers' unique temporal needs. The brainchild of Peter Warhurst, who started a Tampa Bay mini-storage business in 1997, PODS delivers what people on the move crave but rarely get: tranquility in the midst of bedlam.

The centerpiece of this *tempo moderato* approach to moving day is a new wrinkle in the home delivery movement. It's a 960-square-foot cubicle that is dropped off in the driveway of a customer's home. The customer packs furniture and personal items at his own pace, locks up the cubicle, and keeps the keys.

A phone call later, a PODS driver arrives and, using a patented hydraulic lift system, lifts the filled cubicle onto a truck. All this repeats itself in reverse at the destination, where—to everyone's delight—boxes and their contents can be brought into the new house or apartment and unpacked at a civilized pace.

What makes PODS so exciting is that it's a firm that's entraining to its customers' needs, not to its own. It offers a substantial marketing advantage, and apparently is an idea whose time has come. Warhurst and his partners raised $4 million in four days to get PODS off the ground, and franchises are being sold at a record clip.

▋ GETTING IT TOGETHER

Two or more individuals or groups sometimes mesh, regardless of the fact that they are not operating at the same pace. Mentors and protégés, for example, can build strong relationships even though their career stages are temporally distant. Or an R&D group that has dedicated many months to the design of a new product may hand that product over to the marketing department; although the two groups are entrained to very different stages of the product life cycle, their interests still naturally overlap.

This drives alliances and encourages cooperation rather then competition, particularly among firms that are in the early or late stages of development. Consider, for example, a young, untested, but highly creative entrepreneurial start-up (typically unstructured, small, and short of cash) that seeks a linkage with a larger firm (further into the life cycle) that is losing its innovative edge as a result of its size and bureaucracy.

Time masters find ways to entrain even the most divergent of rhythms. Perhaps no example is more illustrative than basketball's Chicago Bulls during the 1990s. The team included some very strong, and very different, personalities. Foremost, of course, was Michael Jordan, whose amazing talent was complemented by an intense work ethic and a sincere desire to win. Operating at a slower, steadier pace was forward Scotty Pippin, who would have been the star of many other teams, but here played something of a supporting role. And then there was Dennis Rodman, the wild, erratic, and moody rebounder *par excellence.* Add the many players who cycled through the team during the decade, and there was clearly great potential for success—or for chaos, if these diverse rhythms could not work together.

Enter head coach Phil Jackson. Quite simply, Jackson was able to achieve this state of harmonic entrainment with the Bulls. This doesn't mean that the players always observed the same rhythm, on the court or off (Rodman alone pretty much precluded that). Instead, Jackson served as conductor of a complex symphony. The players maintained their unique rhythms (individual playing style, sense of urgency, and personality) while working together toward the same goal. And working effectively. The team won six NBA championships under Jackson's leadership. Perhaps even more impressively, Jackson later replicated this success as coach of the Los Angeles Lakers, where he brought that team—including superstars Kobe Bryant and Shaquille O'Neil—into a championship-winning state of harmonic entrainment.

Jackson's secret was deceptively simple. For him, a leader's vision, always important, was absolutely paramount when trying to get people with divergent rhythms to work together. His temporal intelligence enabled him to make all team members—not just the stars—feel like integral parts of the organization:

> My goal was to give everyone on the team a vital role—
> even though I knew I couldn't give every man equal playing time, nor could I change the NBA's disproportionate

system of financial rewards. But I could get the bench players to be more actively involved. My idea was to use ten players regularly and give the others enough playing time so that they could blend in effortlessly with everybody else when they were on the floor.[10]

Time masters embrace the concept of entrainment. They know that ignoring it is to invite failure.

That's exactly what happened recently at Ocean Spray, Inc., the cranberry industry's largest cooperative. Once highly regarded for its marketing acumen (these are the folks who created Cranberry Juice Cocktail, Cran-Apple juice, and those irresistible sweetened dried cranberries called Craisins), it has lately failed to keep pace with consumer buying behavior. Increasingly, juice buyers are eschewing the traditional grocery store shelf and are purchasing their drinks at convenience stores, cafeterias, vending machines, and other "single-service" sources.

Among consumer products companies, mass marketing is a dying art. Customers increasingly want more and more alternatives. Simply put, rapidly changing market forces have overtaken the once powerful and very independent Ocean Spray. Now, lacking both the right distribution system to market single cans and bottles and the financial resources to outpromote the competition, Ocean Spray, Inc. finds itself at a temporal crossroads. As Jim Tillotson, former Ocean Spray board member, told a reporter, "The cruelty of the situation is that the business environment is overtaking [the growers]."[11]

▌ THE KING'S CLOCK

In 1370, King Charles V of France unveiled what was then a revolutionary piece of engineering: a public clock housed in a tower of his palace. (You can still see the clock today in what is now called the Conciergerie, not far from the Cathedral of Notre Dame. See Figure 4-1.) It was the first public clock in Paris, and Charles was quick to see its potential. He issued a decree that all clocks in the city were henceforth to be synchronized with this royal clock, striking the hours at precisely the same time. He had created what the Germans call a *zeitgeber*, or time giver—a temporal cue for the surrounding environment.

As time historian Allen Bluedorn has noted, "This decree effectively made [the] clock the *zeitgeber* for Parisian clocks, and to a certain extent, the *zeitgeber* for general rhythms of life in Paris."[12]

A somewhat more modern example of technology as *zeitgeber* is the Internet, which in many ways has changed the rhythm of how we work. Consider, for example, the temporal impact of e-mail. For many of us, the tempo of electronic communication is hurried, random, and manic. We are sitting at our computer working on a project spreadsheet, when— *da-dong!*—a pleasant chime tells us that we have mail. We immediately invoke our e-mail program to check the message. Perhaps it is a message that interests us; we read it, and maybe we respond. Perhaps it is a message worth reading, but requiring no response. Perhaps it is a message that we want to think about before responding. Perhaps it is just spam, which we curse and delete.

In any event, our project has temporarily faded into the background. We switch back to the spreadsheet, of course, but we may have lost our train of thought. We review the numbers and are just starting to get back into the spreadsheet's rhythm, when again—*da-dong!*—we have mail. We know, logically, that we should resist the temptation to check

Figure 4-1.   The King's Clock. *(Copyright © Dr. Allen Bluedorn, used with permission.)*

it. We need to complete this spreadsheet. But it's so hard. We're like junkies waiting for our next fix. That inbox could contain anything: good news or bad. It's an addiction, one that is easy to deny and easier to shrug off, yet an addiction nonetheless.

For some of us, the technological addiction of choice is information. A colleague of ours keeps a small television on his desk, constantly tuned to a cable news channel. His job does not require real-time awareness of the day's news. But that news ticker at the bottom of the screen is so inviting, so . . . current. If that doesn't provide the requisite level of detail, there's always CNN.com, which will automatically refresh itself so that you are guaranteed to be in the loop every nanosecond. It's a level of information that kings and presidents could not command just a few years ago (during the first Gulf War, Saddam Hussein received his most up-to-date intelligence from CNN). Now many ordinary citizens feel isolated without it.

Staying current and responding to e-mails quickly are not, in and of themselves, bad things. Customers may appreciate the e-mail diligence in particular, as will coworkers and bosses. The question is, though, *at what cost* does this advantage come? Rarely do top executives discussing a manager's performance say, "Rose's group has not been profitable lately . . . on the other hand, she does respond quickly to e-mails!"

Having a high level of temporal intelligence does not mean that you avoid e-mail or cable news programs; instead, you dictate their rhythms. There is no single, universal rhythm for communicating electronically or gathering news reports. We have observed a handful of effective leaders who constantly hover near the Bloomberg terminal or maintain a cyborg-like connection to Microsoft Outlook, yet somehow manage to retain their sanity. But not many. The ones who do tend to be extreme polychronic types who absolutely live for multitasking. And it is true that some jobs—that of an oil trader, for instance—require such split-second awareness of world events.

Yet most of us are not oil traders, and we're more effective if we slow down the tempo at which we receive information. Rather than receiving a constant stream of data (the equivalent of a fast, frenzied drumbeat), we're better off regulating the tempo to a more reasonable, comfortable rhythm. Some people check a news web site every hour or two, and find that perfectly acceptable. Others check up on world events once in the morning and once in the afternoon. Still others actually enjoy waiting for that old (and dying) ritual, the evening paper or the network newscast. Each of us must find the personal rhythm that makes us the most productive. Don't worry—if something truly monumental happens in the world, then the other people on your floor (the ones who are not getting much done) will be sure to tell you about it.

The same goes for e-mail. Of the dozens of messages that may interrupt your day, how many truly have to be seen and acted upon within seconds? How many, in truth, could not wait for an hourly e-mail check, or even a once-a-morning and once-an-afternoon check? (Besides, jumping every time the bell rings, like Pavlov's dogs, just isn't civilized.)

Some leaders choose to ignore the *zeitgeber* of the Internet altogether. Love him or hate him, one of Donald Trump's more intriguing traits is that he simply refuses to be a slave to technology. He is in constant communication with his key employees, yet he always meets them face to face or communicates by telephone, never by e-mail. According to a *Fortune* reporter who trailed Trump for a time, "The only computer in his office sits unplugged, on a windowsill."[13]

Of course, if you are a midlevel production manager, such a lifestyle choice may not be feasible. Try telling the boss, "I'm temporally enlightened now, and will no longer be a slave to my inbox. Communicate with me in other ways from now on. I'll respond at the end of the day." You're likely to have more time on your hands than you expected.

Maybe it's not such a bad idea, though, to emulate the spirit of what Trump and others like him are doing. Sure, most of us aren't billionaires who can choose which social conventions we'll accept; we don't have an army of assistants to handle everyday details like personal communication. Most of us would not be well served by ignoring e-mail altogether, but we can dictate the tempo of communication. It's up to us whether we will simply be swept along by these electronic rhythms, or whether we will become the conductor.

■ LEADERS AS *ZEITGEBERS*

Every organization is subject to numerous *external rhythms* that dictate how we do business. On the broadest level, economic cycles are *zeitgebers* that entrain us to the outside world. If you manufacture air conditioners, then the seasons are important *zeitgebers*, affecting new product introductions, production schedules, and perhaps even the size of your workforce. For public companies, quarters are *zeitgebers*, instigating not only a flurry of reporting but often the actual timing of business decisions.

Organizations are also subject to *internal rhythms* that reflect how we do business. Budget cycles can be powerful *zeitgebers.* So can weekly meetings or periodic messages from the CEO.

Unfortunately, internal *zeitgebers* aren't always positive. The fiscal year end, for example, prompts a near-universal dominating—and sometimes detrimental—rhythm that is entrained into the financial fabric of nearly all organizations. The impact of this seemingly innocuous temporal tradition, meant simply to define the beginning and end of an accounting period, is significant and widespread.

June 30, September 30, or whatever, the close of an organization's fiscal year entrains everything around it. Personnel evaluations. Pricing changes. Salary and bonus adjustments. In the worst case, even the improper manipulation of revenue. (The fiscal year convention actually enabled the Enron debacle; the energy conglomerate's whiz kids set up dummy businesses that passed bookkeeping entries back and forth through successive fiscal years.)

Time masters understand that they, themselves, can become either positive or negative *zeitgebers*, setting the rhythm for those around them.

Consider one company we observed, where showing up for work on time was apparently a lifestyle choice. The people were talented and not necessarily given to laziness, but few felt much urgency of purpose. Lunches were long, languid affairs with plenty of side trips for shopping—even movies. Yet at 5:00 in the afternoon, you could almost feel the breeze caused by people rushing for the elevators. The firm was number four in its industry, and that felt just fine to most employees.

In response, a series of executives decided to take decisive action to remind employees of their responsibilities. They instituted a series of mechanical *zeitgebers*. The lunch hour was officially shortened to half an hour. Sign-in sheets were required for salaried employees, and time cards for hourly employees, in an effort to control time.

This was all nominally successful. In fact, most people now arrived at work precisely at 7:59 a.m.—one minute before the official start time. But in this adversarial environment, few arrived any earlier. People learned quickly to play the system. They found new, creative ways to limit their productivity. Forgery of colleagues' signatures was rumored. An us/them corporate culture makes it easy to rationalize almost any type of behavior and to sleep very well at night, thank you.

But one day the president of the company took a different approach. He became a human *zeitgeber*. An affable man, he started to greet employees in the building's lobby each morning. Soon the throng of people at 7:59 was slightly smaller; some began to arrive at 7:30 so that the president would notice their ambition. A few started to arrive even earlier, just to see how early the old man got there himself. (No one ever found out; some suspected that he secretly lived somewhere in the building.)

The employees all knew what he was doing, of course. At the same time, they knew that they should be working harder. A leader with a stiffer personality probably could not have pulled it off. But this was a welcome *zeitgeber*; many people were looking for reasons to work harder. They became entrained to his rhythm. Along with other initiatives, such as more logical incentive plans, the renewed work ethic soon helped the company overtake its nearest competitor. Long after the president retired, the company retained its more vibrant rhythm.

Corporate rhythms are about much more than just the

length of the workday, however. And *zeitgebers* do not necessarily come from the highest levels of management.

For instance, imagine yourself as a new marketing analyst for a health maintenance organization. You have been asked to study consumer perceptions of three hospitals used by the HMO—an understandable enough task. The marketing staff is small, though, and your boss offers you no specific guidance. She figures that business school must have taught you something.

But while school may have given you many of the necessary skills for such a project, it did precious little to teach you about issues of appropriate *timing*. How long should it take to complete such a project properly? A day? A week? A month? You don't want to seem like an idiot, so you probably won't ask such a basic question. So how do you proceed? Most likely, you complete the project on the assumption that your task is important, that time is of the essence. We all like to think so. You work hard, and within two weeks you submit an insightful report, succinct but thorough.

Now you wait for feedback. It is at this point that your boss becomes a powerful, and perhaps unwitting, *zeitgeber.* If the report arrives back quickly with comments (and perhaps even encouraging remarks), then you will no doubt get to work right away on your next project. Even in the absence of overt temporal cues, you will assume that the work tempo you have set, the project rhythm, is appropriate.

On the other hand, if after many days you still haven't heard back, then you will draw some obvious conclusions about the importance of your work. Apparently the tempo of this HMO's marketing department is not allegro (lively) but adagio (slow; the root word in Latin actually means "convenient"). You can play adagio, if that's what the conductor wants. This is entrainment, but of an unwelcome sort.

This evokes memories of Parkinson's Law—the idea that work expands (or contracts) to fill the time available. Temporal studies confirm the simple truth of this. When given progressively more time to accomplish tasks, people deliberately slack off. In one study, subjects who were given five, then ten, then finally twenty minutes to solve anagram puzzles quickly became entrained to a much slower pace. Fortunately, this tendency also works in the other direction. When time is short, tempo entrainment can get an organization moving and shaking as it drives individuals and teams to adapt to those frenetic outside temporal conditions. Members "get the beat," matching their speed to the pace and tempo of their environment.

Leaders—whether CEOs, middle managers, or line foremen—are constantly providing temporal cues to those around them. These cues often have little to do with temporal keywords like *cycle, speed,* or *deadline.* But they do much to determine, for better or worse, an organization's rhythm.

▌ NEW RHYTHMS AT 3M

The power of rhythm has been described beautifully by Shona Brown and Kathleen Eisenhardt in their book *Competing on the Edge.* They assert that rhythm (they call it *time pacing*) has been a prime success driver at Minnesota-based 3M, where multimillion-dollar earners like Scotchgard (a researcher accidentally spilled a strong chemical on her tennis shoes) and Post-it Notes (originally a solution for keeping an employee's church hymnal organized) were created.

According to Brown and Eisenhardt, such 3M success stories are the result of an intentional internal rhythm that drives the momentum for change, enabling 3M to create and then introduce hundreds of successful new products every year.

Such time pacing is not about tempo or speed—at 3M, the rhythmic pattern remains the same no matter what the tempo. The company's leaders seem to know the right rhythm and communicate it throughout the organization. "This simple rule," observe Brown and Eisenhardt, "sets the rhythm of change, from past to present to future, for the entire corporation."[14]

And like those notations that establish the cadence in music (4/4 time, say, or 3/4 waltz time), 3M's beat is set by the numbers. For many years, 3M operated at what we'd call 3/10 time. The rule was that new products must account for *at least 30 percent of total sales* each year. Just as good golfers know that a smooth, accurate swing depends upon a consistent and repeatable cadence (that sought-after state of being "in the groove" or "in the zone"), 3M's leaders understood that timing and 3/10 rhythm were important competitive advantages. And, as in music, it is rhythm—leadership's movement in time—that provides harmony, momentum, and achievement.

Simply put, at 3M, leadership is very much a temporal art. Its leaders' performances take place *in* time. But those unique 3M rhythms are made up *of* time. The point is that time not only provides the *means* by which the performance occurs, but also becomes the *substance* and the idea of that performance. Like virtuosos, these leaders *keep* the time while also having the ability to change the temporal characteristics of their performance at a moment's notice.

This has happened at 3M, where, since December 2000, there has been a new conductor at the podium. CEO James McNerney's change of rhythm has been nothing short of revolutionary. Out is the quirky 3/10 rhythm that made inno-vation at any price part of the cultural norm. In its place, McNerney has begun conducting with an entirely new beat, one designed to bring economic Darwinism to 3M's innova-tive free-for-all.

Only new ideas with $100 million market potential make the cut. The idea is to halve the time it takes to get new 3M products into the marketplace. McNerney calls this "accelera-tion." Musically speaking, we'd call it presto. Happily, 3M's fresh and very intentional rhythm, its slightly faster cultural metronome, still permeates everything the firm does. And everyone in the company hears its ubiquitous beat.

Clearly, the idea that rhythm counts in leadership has caught on. Case Western Reserve professor Lauretta McLeod and her colleague, Steven Freeman of the University of Penn-sylvania, for example, are harnessing the haunting beat of the Argentine tango to parallel the skills required to be an effec-tive leader. A dance with no predetermined choreography, the tango is an apt metaphor for all sorts of leader behaviors: spontaneity in thinking, improvisation, leading and following simultaneously, and creativity.

The dance is also the *text* for Freeman and McLeod's semi-nars on leadership. Building on the notion that savvy leaders respond to rhythms within their organizations, participants are asked to interpret the insistent beat of tango music. This leads to listening to the interpretations of others' takes on what is to many an unfamiliar rhythm. Inevitably, a discus-sion of improvisation emerges.

Then the dance begins. There are rules. Argentine tango is an education in living in the moment. It requires that you manage your mind, body, and spirit. At each step, your awareness of the floor, your partner, and the music must be absolute. Freeman and McLeod (who've been dancing the tango together for two years) put it this way: "The dance must be within the tempo, feeling, and flow of the music; each couple must move in time with other couples around them; and the partners must be in constant dialogue with each other." Accomplishing this requires the capacity to influence others and quickly reveals the dynamics of the leader-follower relationship.[15]

Getting the right rhythm requires walking in the other person's *temporal shoes*. Only when people share the same rhythm do they *really* connect with each other, establishing a relationship that is both fascinating and productive. The great basketball player Bill Russell can serve as a role model here. In his autobiography, *Second Wind*, he describes those moments when he and his team played at their very best. Perhaps unknowingly, his teammates would become so entrained to the rhythm of the game that the score no longer mattered. It was the remarkable rhythm that counted.[16]

Rhythm is one of the main regulating principles of communication and organizational success, playing a critical role in an organization's trajectory.

So bring on the drums. Let the dance begin!

■ HOW YOU CAN APPLY TEMPORAL INTELLIGENCE

Here are some actions you can take to optimize the rhythms of your team:

- ■ Leverage your team's or your organization's existing rhythms. Understand that each company, each department, each team has a rhythm of its own.

The way you make that rhythm converge with other organizational rhythms can determine your success or failure.

- Harness the power of entrainment to create new organizational rhythms. You can change the pace of things by synchronizing existing rhythms and creating new ones.

- Lead polychronically. Tolerate—and even enjoy—a highly fragmented business day, full of variety and interruptions. An example: Promote a work climate in which people feel free to enter your office space without an appointment, even if it disrupts what is going on. Sure, this violates time management principles, but that's the point.

- Make an inventory of the *zeitgebers*, or external pacers, that drive the rhythms of your organization. Which ones are no longer relevant? You'll generally find these among the organization's mindlessly recurring activities that have long since lost their relevance. It's best to jettison them as soon as possible.

CHAPTER 5

IT'S GREEK TO ME:
CHRONOS AND *KAIROS*

ANY SAILOR who has left port on a breezy day knows a very special kind of temporal transition that comes when you leave the shore and enter the sea. First, time speeds by. There is the thrill that comes just as you leave the harbor and motor out. With only the sea in front of you, you turn into the wind, add power to the engine, and hoist the sails, hauling them in to reduce rolling. You look at your watch, calculating speed, distance, and time, figuring that this chaos will last another five minutes. You feel the boat complain as it crawls away from shore, falling off course, pitching and yawing wildly. The sails whip back and forth. A burst of engine power gives you just enough control to slowly turn out of the eye of the wind. You figure another two minutes.

You're not thinking about sailing, you're thinking about the clock.

Suddenly everything changes. The sails fill with wind and are finally taut and still—"sleeping," as sailors put it. You turn off the engine. Its noisy *thrunk thrunk* is replaced by the sound of seawater sluicing past the hull. The boat yields to the wind and heels over slightly. It's almost sailing itself. Time is no longer in control; it has stopped. This is the perfect moment. You're sailing.

You have just experienced two entirely different senses of time, as did the ancient Greeks.

The first they named *chronos*, for Zeus's father, one of the Titans. *Chronos'* most common emblems are the watch you wear and the clock on the wall. Both remind us constantly that time is a very limited asset, one that must be used sparingly; that we all live in a sequential universe in which each minute inexorably follows the previous one. While waiting for the minutes to pass as you motored toward the open sea, you were on *chronos* time.

Chronos is a temporal measuring device that comes down to us by custom and usage, the special needs of bureaucracy, governance, and necessity. *Chronos* has given its contours to business, social mores, and technology since ancient times. Its manifestations, clocks and calendars, have unwittingly enforced a discernible and simplistic pattern in the flow of time. *Chronos* aficionados have created everything from wall calendars to PDAs to devices that rudely wake us up (one of the most notable was an alarm clock bed that tipped its unfortunate occupant onto the floor at a predetermined time). No wonder the American philosopher and writer Lewis Mumford concluded that "the clock, not the steam engine, is the key machine of the modern industrial age."[1] And social anthropologist John Postill underscores our time obsession. "Chronos and its manifestation, clock and calendar time, may not make the world go round, but it . . . is the invisible hand of the market, state and civil society alike."[2]

But the Greeks believed that there was another kind of time, one very different from *chronos*. This they named *kairos*, after Zeus's youngest son. *Kairos* is not concerned with minutes, hours, or days, but with the "right time," the point at which everything changes—when that sailboat takes on a life of its own. Think of a kairotic moment as one that marks an opportunity, a point of departure.

The concept of *kairos* was so revered by Pythagoras (he of the famous geometry theorem $a^2 + b^2 = c^2$) and his followers that they assigned a sort of mystical significance to it. Applied to rhetoric, *kairos* referred to the decisive point in an argument, a spontaneous or creative verbal thrust by the speaker. It was the job of the skilled rhetorician to recognize the kairotic moment, and to strike at just that point—not before and not after.

The essence of *kairos* is found in the Old Testament, perhaps most famously in this passage from *Ecclesiastes*:

> To everything there is a season, and a time to every purpose under the heaven: a time to be born, and a time to die; a time to plant, and a time to pluck up that which is planted; a time to kill, and a time to heal . . . a time to weep and a time to laugh.

(The link is even stronger in the New Testament, which was originally written in Greek; the very first sentence reportedly uttered by Jesus Christ after his baptism actually includes the word *kairos*—translated in the King James version as "The time [*kairos*] is fulfilled, and the kingdom of God is at hand.")

John E. Smith, a Yale professor whose unabashed goal is the rehabilitation of this kairotic aspect of time, differentiates *kairos* from *chronos* in the following way:

> The questions relative to [*chronos*] are: "How fast?" "How frequent?" "How old?" and the answers to these questions can be given in cardinal numbers. . . . By contrast, the term *kairos* points to a *qualitative* character of time, to the special position an event or action occupies in a series, to a season when something appropriately happens that cannot just happen at "any time," but only at *that* time, to a time that marks a possibility which may not recur. The question especially relevant to *kairos* is "When?" "At what time?"[3]

■ SO HOW DOES THIS HELP ME NEXT TUESDAY?

Let's leave the dusty hallways of antiquity and consider how these two kinds of time, *chronos* and *kairos*, affect the way we lead. Along the way, you will discover how understanding them can increase your temporal intelligence.

It's not at all difficult to describe how *chronos* manifests itself in our world. Look around you: watches, calendars, day planners, Palm Pilots, Gantt charts, project management software . . . not to mention most time management books and seminars. But how do we move *beyond* time management, beyond *chronos*?

What does *kairos* look like in our world?

Consider your personal experience with kairotic time. Think of a moment when, regardless of what the clock or the calendar said, it simply *felt like the right time* to do something. Here are some examples—some seemingly minor, some with profound implications:

- You suddenly decide that a junior analyst is ready to become a manager, and you promote her well ahead of schedule.

- You decide to increase your factory's capacity even though the raw numbers seem to suggest otherwise.

- Your gut tells you that the high-end product with the great margins is about to turn into a dog; much to the surprise of your colleagues (and your competition), you change your strategy.

- You realize that you'd better stop talking and start listening to that employee who disagrees with you.

- You somehow "feel it in your bones" that it's time to quit your job and start your own firm.

The kairotic moment usually isn't apparent beforehand. For instance, we recently attended the inauguration ceremony of a new college president. The ceremony was not particularly long, as these things go, but there were plenty of speakers: students, faculty, members of the community, representatives from other colleges, the keynote speaker . . . by the time the new president rose to speak, there had probably been a dozen speakers, whose speeches had ranged from two minutes to twenty.

When the new president, for whom this event existed, finally walked to the podium, he looked up at the audience, then down at his speech. Understandably, he had spent many hours crafting his planned remarks. This was certainly one of the most important events of his life; that speech was the stuff of daydreams. The audience waited quietly, anticipating the usual long inaugural speech.

It didn't happen. Instead, the president looked up again at the audience. "I have a prepared speech," he said, "but I'm not going to give it." He certainly could have; the respectful audience would have stayed, no matter how long the speech lasted. Yet he sensed that it was time to do something else. In an instant, he considered the tone and substance of his remarks, gauged them against the speeches that had come before, and evaluated the mood of the audience. He decided, based on his temporal intelligence, that the time was not right for his carefully crafted speech. Instead, he made some short, spontaneous remarks about how glad he was to be there, how warm the college community's reception had been, and how excited he was about the future.

And then the ceremony was over. The president's conversational remarks contrasted sharply with the sort of canned, general speech the audience had expected. Having girded themselves for perhaps the longest speech of the day, the audience members now felt absolutely refreshed. The president had judged this kairotic moment correctly. People came away energized by his short but significant remarks, and talked about them for some time afterward.

Chances are you have seen people make such kairotic decisions—or have made some yourself. Interestingly, if you ask people why they took the action they did when they did, they will probably say, "I don't know. It just seemed like the right thing to do at the time." They seem to have a kairotic sense of timing.

Some people dismiss this as luck. But it's much more than that.

■ KAIROTIC CLOCKS

In his book *The Lonely Crowd*, sociologist and lawyer David Riesman famously suggested that "inner-directed" people tend to be self-motivated, goal-oriented, and led by their own unique sense of mission. They apparently have a kind of sixth sense that gives them near-perfect timing. Not surprisingly, Riesman predicted that "inner-directed" types would be the most likely to assume leadership roles in organizations and in society.

Each of us, it turns out, has within us an amazing time-piece—a kairotic clock that can act, if we let it, as a temporal guide. The key is learning how to read this kairotic clock accurately and mustering the courage to rely on it.

One of our favorite fictional examples occurs in the film *The Hunt for Red October*. In this film, a Russian submarine captain named Ramius (played by Sean Connery) commands a huge submarine in the North Atlantic. Traveling at almost sixty miles per hour, the submarine banks gracefully, first to starboard and then to port, just missing underwater mountain peaks on either side. The submarine's navigator, after checking his stopwatch, casually announces that the next turn in this underwater abyss will come in precisely 6 minutes, 30 seconds.

All of this seems routine until several minutes later, when a half-ton torpedo acquires the submarine and unrelentingly homes in. The crew's attempts to confuse the torpedo work briefly, but it soon reacquires the submarine and rushes onward, a shark sensing blood. There is no escape for the sub, no room to maneuver. Trying to outrun its pursuer, it is trapped between two jagged cliffs.

The only hope is to make the turn before the steadily gaining torpedo hits. The navigator urgently begins his countdown.

"Four . . . three . . . two . . . one . . . mark!"

Yet the submarine captain does nothing.

"The turn, Captain!" The navigator's voice is insistent.

An underwater Matterhorn looms dead ahead; a collision is imminent. Yet the captain seems not to care. He is somewhere else.

"Captain, we are out of the lane!" the navigator exclaims.

But the captain is not listening. Apart from a slight change in his breathing, he shows no particular emotion. His lips move almost imperceptibly, as if he is talking to himself. He's processing information. That is clear. But he is also "seeing" something that no one else sees. He's on kairotic time.

Finally, milliseconds before the submarine collides with the escarpment, the captain shouts, "Right full rudder! Reverse starboard engine!" The immense submarine shudders as its rudder and right propeller force it into an emergency turn, and it misses the cliff face by mere yards. The torpedo explodes into the rocks.

Clearly the captain knew a thing or two about driving a submarine. Yet what really saved the day was his exquisite sense of timing and his ability to recognize a kairotic moment. Call it what you will: gut feel, intuition, sixth sense. Something told him to turn at that precise moment, not before and not after.

▮ *KAIROS* AT WORK

Most business schools teach students to break down complex problems into bite-sized chunks that lend themselves to quantitative measurement. Need to make an important decision? Find a whiteboard and start drawing fishbone diagrams. Assign probabilities and expected values to various scenarios. Then simply multiply the probabilities by the expected values and choose the option with the highest expected net present value!

Words are often regarded with suspicion—but numbers don't lie. As Mr. Gradgrind says in the opening of Charles Dickens's *Hard Times*:

> Now, what I want is, Facts. Teach these boys and girls nothing but Facts. Facts alone are wanted in life. Plant nothing else, and root out everything else. You can only form the minds of reasoning animals upon Facts: nothing else will ever be of any service to them. This is the principle on which I bring up my own children, and this is the principle on which I bring up these children. Stick to the Facts, Sir![4]

The trouble is, sometimes facts alone—as in the case of that giant submarine—prove to be insufficient, or lead us astray, or lead to paralysis by analysis. "Decoding the creative process and assigning values to the various components may be comforting to people who have no marketing instincts," cautions advertising executive Andy Dumaine, "but it is counter-productive and anti-business."[5]

It certainly doesn't seem like the way most of us make important *personal* decisions. There is an old story about a business professor who receives a job offer from another school. Not sure what to do, he asks a colleague for guidance. The colleague is quick to offer advice. "Just do what you teach," he says. "Write down the pros and cons, attach weights and probabilities, and maximize your subjective utility."

The professor scoffs. "Don't be silly. This decision is serious."[6]

In fairness, some people do make personal decisions with this type of analytical rigor. One of us recalls a former colleague who, when searching for a new house, visited fifty potential properties. She then created an Excel spreadsheet rating each property on eleven dimensions, including commute time, kitchen quality, the size of the yard, and so on. She assigned each property a 0 to 10 score on each dimension and determined a percentage weight for each dimension. Commute time, for instance, counted twice as much as price per square foot. She bought the house with the highest overall numerical score.

The truth is, though, few of us make important life decisions with spreadsheets or complex fishbone diagrams. So why do we tend to assume that such analysis is *de rigueur* for business decisions?

Increasingly, the subject of *kairos* has been gaining attention in the world of management. There are books and articles on the subject, and even "kairotic consultants" who, for a fee, will help your company connect with its kairotic side.[7] Some of this is no doubt humbug (trust us; we just feel it in our bones). For one thing, gut feel and intuition are often wrong. For another, plenty of people who simply haven't done their homework like to hide behind false veils of creativity.

Be that as it may, there really does seem to be something to *kairos*, intuition, and good business decisions.

Two researchers, Greg A. Stevens and James Burley, have studied the impact of such kairotic thinking on new product development, a notoriously difficult activity (of those products that make it to market, only around 60 percent ever prove financially successful—and that's not counting the much larger number that never make it to market at all). Stevens and Burley spent ten years interviewing hundreds of managers for a global *Fortune* 500 chemical manufacturer. Over that ten-year period, the company launched 267 new products. Stevens and Burley tracked the financial success of all 267 products, but they were also particularly interested in the *individual analysts* who had evaluated and overseen those product concepts early in the development process. They call this early stage, in which new ideas are first seriously vetted, the "fuzzy front end" of the new product development process.

Stevens and Burley hypothesized that there might be personality differences between analysts with successful and unsuccessful new product track records. They administered the Myers-Briggs Type Indicator to the analysts. The four major Myers-Briggs dichotomies are:

Extraversion ↔ Introversion

Sensing ↔ Intuition

Thinking ↔ Feeling

Perceiving ↔ Judging

The results were striking. On two of the Myers-Briggs dichotomies, Extraversion/Introversion and Perceiving/Judging, Stevens and Burley found no statistically significant differences between those analysts who were good at shepherding successful new products and those who weren't. But on the other two dichotomies, the successful analysts exhibited a very strong preference for Intuition (N) and Thinking (T).

In fact, those analysts who scored high on Intuition and Thinking were *much* more likely to create money-making product launches. Analysts ranking in the top third on the NT scale earned *95 times more profit* for the company than those analysts in the lower third, and nine times more than those analysts in the middle third of the NT scale![8]

What exactly *are* Intuition and Thinking in Myers-Briggs parlance? The official definitions are:

> *Sensing* and *Intuition* describe how people like to take in information and what kind of information they tend to trust. In other words, do you notice and give more weight to information that comes in through your five senses (Sensing) or do you give more weight to information that is assigned meaning and patterns (Intuition)?
>
> *Thinking* and *Feeling* describe how a person likes to make decisions about the information taken in using either Sensing or Intuition. Do you give more weight to objective principles and impersonal facts (Thinking) or to personal human concerns, and people issues (Feeling)?[9]

This Intuition-Thinking combination is quite interesting, because it involves absorbing information in a kairotic way, but actually making decisions based on objective principles and (perhaps Mr. Gradgrind was half right after all) cold, hard facts.

This may seem incongruous, but it isn't. Good kairotic thinkers—at least the kind we're talking about—are not just pulling things out of the air, not just relying on luck. They are, above all, pattern finders. In his book *Sources of Power*, Gary Klein studied decision makers who have to make good decisions under intense time pressures, people like triage nurses or firefighters. He found that they rarely use complex decision models. Instead, they see patterns, things that remind them of other things. They make a decision because it just seems right, based on their experience.[10]

In other words, they are *gathering information* by identifying patterns, consciously or unconsciously. But this in no way precludes their making use of facts and objective principles when these are available to help guide their decisions.

They use both sides of the brain . . .

▌ CONTRARIANS

. . . As did Barry Cottle, Palm Inc.'s co-chief operating officer. In 2002, Cottle decided to leave Palm and start a new business venture in Silicon Valley. This might not seem unusual—except that the high-tech industry was in the middle of a historic economic downturn. Not surprisingly, Cottle was surrounded by naysayers, including members of his family. His timing, they insisted, could not have been worse.

As Cottle told a *Wall Street Journal* reporter, however, something told him that the time was ripe. He put his family on a tight budget, moved them to less-expensive Atlanta, and started up Mobile Digital Media, Inc., a company that makes multimedia cards that add extra memory and content to handheld computers. Cottle's timing was more adroit than he had expected. He now has thirteen people on his staff, he's closed a first round of financing, and Mobile Digital will soon clear $25 million in revenue.

Frank Lanza, a defense industry executive, decided to start a company called L-3 Communications at what seemed the worst possible time. It was 1997, and the government's defense budget had been down for a decade. A wave of consolidations had left only a handful of $10 billion-plus giant contractors. Domestic concerns were at the top of the list in Washington, and all the brightest engineers had left for Silicon Valley. Everyone was bailing out.

No matter. Lanza listened to his kairotic clock, went against the crowd (he knew that there'd always be a defense industry), and bought ten down-and-out divisions from his former employer for $500 million. Today, L-3's products are used in reconnaissance, surveillance, and communication technology. Since going public in 1998, the company's stock has more than tripled, resulting in a recent valuation of $3.4 billion. That internal clock, that "gut feel"—as any contrarian investor will tell you—can help transform a downturn into a bonanza.

People like Cottle, Lanza, and the fictitious Captain Ramius often employ their kairotic clocks to guide them, and as a result, they do the opposite of what is expected. They see a situation quite differently from the way others see it, knowing that a combination of experience and gut feel can often result in exquisite timing and the ability to make changes in course at just the right moment.

■ CHASING *KAIROS*: INTEL CORPORATION AND STRATEGIC INFLECTION POINTS

Every once in a while something *big* happens that changes everything. While the ancient Greeks called such moments kairotic, Intel chairman Andy Grove calls them *strategic inflection points.*

Simple inflection points are mathematical phenomena. For those among us who remember college calculus, an inflection point is the point where a curve's second derivative changes sign from positive to negative, or vice versa. Got it? For the rest of us, it's helpful to see a graphic example, so take a look at Figure 5-1.

The inflection point, then, is the point at which the curve changes from concave to convex or from convex to concave. It's the point at which things change.

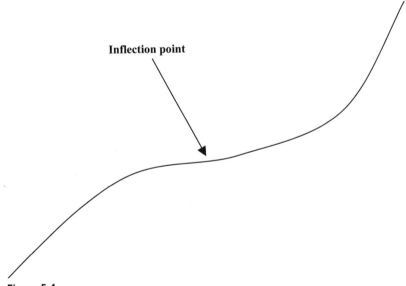

Figure 5-1.

What does this have to do with leadership? Everything.

Grove is obsessed with strategic inflection points, as is evident in his book *Only the Paranoid Survive*. He describes them this way:

> When exactly does a strategic inflection point take place? It's hard to pinpoint, even in retrospect. Picture yourself going on a hike with a group of friends and getting lost. Some worrywart in the group will be the first one to ask the leader, "Are you sure you know where we're going? Aren't we lost?" The leader will wave him away and march on. But then the uneasiness over lack of trail markers or other familiar signs will grow and at some point the leader will reluctantly stop in his tracks, scratch his head and admit, not too happily, "Hey, guys, I think we *are* lost." The business equivalent of that moment is the strategic inflection point.[11]

A strategic inflection point, then, is a watershed moment, a major turning point. It can affect an individual, a business, an industry, or a country.

Some inflection points are self-evident. For an individual, the birth of a child often represents an inflection point. (If you have children and your social life didn't change after their birth, please share your secret.) For the owner of a small hardware store, it might be the arrival of Home Depot in town—nothing will ever be the same for you. For an industry, it might be the advent of some new technology, such as the DVD player. For a country, it might be a change of government or a war. Whatever the case, you ignore these inflection points at your peril.

From a business standpoint, it's not always so easy to

know that you are at or near an inflection point. Long after "talkies" had appeared, for example, Charlie Chaplin still believed that silent films would continue to dominate Hollywood. Blinded by his own love of the silent genre, he couldn't see what the rest of the world saw quite clearly: that the days of silent films were numbered. Chaplin conceded only in 1940, with his film *The Great Dictator*—years after the rest of Hollywood had responded to the advent of cinematic sound. To get a sense of just how late Chaplin was to change, recall that this was after *Gone With the Wind, The Wizard of Oz,* and hundreds of other movies had successfully tested the science and the popularity of sound. Chaplin had been the undisputed king of silent film; he never achieved great success in the new genre.

Like Chaplin, Intel faced a major strategic inflection point in its industry. Intel's story provides an important case study in identifying strategic inflection points.

Intel began in 1968 as a manufacturer of computer memory chips. Its first product was a 64-bit memory chip, which could store a total of just 64 digits. The company enjoyed a virtual monopoly in this market until the early 1970s, when a handful of American companies began to manufacture similar chips. The dynamics of the market changed with the entrance of these new competitors, but Intel saw no need to alter its business model. At the time, Intel also had another, smaller business unit that made microprocessors—chips that performed calculations rather than stored data. In 1981, Intel microprocessors had been designed into the first IBM personal computers, whose initial success seemed quite promising.

As the 1980s progressed, though, the situation became more troubling. Intel began to face tough competition from

Japanese memory-chip makers. The Japanese were investing millions of dollars in research and development, and were reportedly working on chips with many times the capacity of Intel's chips. To make matters worse, the quality of the Japanese chips was actually better than that of any American manufacturer. With more supply on the memory chip market, prices and margins began to suffer badly. The Japanese seemed willing to buy market share at any cost. Intel was losing money on memory chips, its bread and butter.

Grove was uneasy, but he didn't know what to do. He was not concerned with terms like *strategic inflection point,* but he knew that something important was happening in the industry. Finally, one day in 1985, Grove walked into the office of Intel's then-CEO, Gordon Moore. Grove asked Moore a provocative question, one that would change Intel (and the world of computing) forever: "If we got kicked out and the board brought in a new CEO, what do you think he would do?"

Moore immediately answered, "He would get us out of memories."

It was a shocking answer. Intel had started as a maker of memory chips; its plant, its equipment, and its identity were tied to memory. Grove knew that this was a fundamental, and frightening, suggestion. Yet he understood Moore's reasoning. "Why shouldn't you and I walk out the door, come back and do it ourselves?" Grove asked.[12]

Ultimately, that's what they did. By mid-1986, Intel was essentially out of the memory business, concentrating its energy on the microprocessor market. This was a stunning shift, somewhat like Ford Motor Company deciding to abandon cars and concentrate on motorcycles. Of course, Intel did pretty well with its new strategy. The world might never have

known the 386, 486, Pentium, Centrino, or Xeon chips if
Grove and Moore had not asked themselves tough questions
and had the vision and audacity to rethink their entire business model. Had they stubbornly clung to the memory business, Intel would probably have been lost in the shuffle, just
one name among dozens.

Recognizing the industry's strategic inflection point—its
kairotic moment—made all the difference for Intel. Grove
and Moore had known for some time that the market was
changing, but it wasn't until they asked themselves some difficult and creative questions that they realized that they had
reached a kairotic moment.

We suggest a slight modification of Grove's courageous
question, one that may help you decide whether you have
reached the kairotic moment in your industry (or business or
project). The next time you suspect that you may be facing
an important turning point, ask yourself this:

> If I had just started my job today, and had inherited this
> project/product/company, what would I do?

Would you invest more time and money in it? Would you
modify its scope? Would you sell it? Would you abandon it?

Such questioning requires you to pull yourself *out of time.*
You may actually have worked at your firm for twelve years,
but you need to forget that fact for a moment and imagine
that you have just walked through the door for the first time.
Temporarily forget all of the history, the insider knowledge,
the loyalty, the baggage you have. Face the situation with
new eyes. Challenge others to answer the same time-bending
question: What would they do?

If, after such questioning, the project at hand still seems

like a good idea, then maybe it is. But if you honestly think you would not pursue the project or the line of business or the industry—or if you and your colleagues find the question particularly agonizing or divisive—then you very well may be facing a strategic inflection point. The time may be right to take decisive action. This has nothing to do with *chronos*— with the clock, the calendar, or whether you're near the end of a fiscal year—and everything to do with *kairos*, the right moment.

Of course, if you decide that the moment is kairotic, there is no guarantee that you will be correct. To make matters worse, you may not know the truth for months, or even years, afterward. There is no magic bullet, no reliable test beyond asking the right questions. But Grove cautions against waiting until you *know* for sure what to do—by that point, it's probably too late. "Timing," he reminds us, "is everything."[13]

▍ DEADLINES

Clearly, due dates can be useful and appropriate tools. Obsession with them, however, often reveals a dangerous tendency to exceed the speed limit.

Consider Great Britain at the end of World War II. Eager to shed itself of its former empire, Britain's impatience and self-imposed deadlines had serious, long-term negative consequences. The bulldog Churchillian resolution that had enabled England to stand alone against the Nazis in the early dark days of the war was replaced by fecklessness and bad timing. Churchill's successor, Labor Party Prime Minister Clement Atlee, engineered an all-too-rapid retreat from empire that bred chaos from New Delhi to Jerusalem. Britain's haste caused the death and displacement of millions of Muslims and Hindus and sowed the seeds of the Arab-Israeli war that so distresses the world today.

The villain in this disaster was not Atlee or his foreign minister, Ernest Bevin. It was the ironclad deadline they had set: August 15, 1947. As Larry Collins and Dominique Lapierre report in *Freedom at Midnight*, a chronicle of the partition of India and Pakistan, not even Lord Mountbatten, the last viceroy of India, could delay this arbitrary timetable. As a result, Muslims and Hindus massacred each other as they attempted to flee across the soon-to-be-official border.

The lesson here, of course, is about the dangers of inflexible schedules.

Yet the lesson was not learned. The British fixation with sticking to timetables quickly led to even more geopolitical folly. Only a year later, they stuck stubbornly to their scheduled withdrawal from Palestine after drawing a map of the region that made the partition of India seem rational in comparison. So started the bitter Arab-Israeli war that still rages today.

As we pointed out in Chapter 2, such *deadlinitis* often disappoints. Although conventional wisdom says that deadlines focus the intellect, they often lead instead to rash, costly decisions. In politics and in business, false deadlines don't break real deadlocks.

■ ODE TO *CHRONOS*

It may seem as if we are trying to discredit *chronos* in favor of *kairos*. Yet nothing could be further from the truth.

In fact, like the Greeks, we accept *chronos* as a necessary condition for *kairos*—as self-evidently important. Who could argue that a successful leader does not need to accept certain realities of the calendar, or the clock? Try submitting your company's next 10-K report to the SEC a few weeks late, explaining simply, "We lost track of the time." Try walking into your next board meeting an hour late, saying, "It just didn't feel like the right moment for me to arrive." Try returning calls to important clients only when the spirit moves you. You're welcome to try any of these strategies; just be sure you know the directions to your nearest unemployment office.

Whether we like it or not, the world runs on clocks and calendars. Yet it is possible to be successful without becoming a *slave* to *chronos*.

We recently met with a group of fifteen regional managers for a large corporation. Most were still in their thirties; they were clearly up-and-comers in the organization, already making hundreds of thousands of dollars a year. These folks were experts at managing *chronos*. They were *chronos* gunfighters. The tools of their trade hung from their belts like six-shooters: personal digital assistants, cell phones, pagers, BlackBerries. And they weren't afraid to use them. Every few minutes the table would shake: Someone's PDA, or cell phone, or pager, or BlackBerry had just rung in vibrate mode. Fourteen pairs of eyes would quickly dart to the table, where they had placed their precious devices, to see if the message was for them. More often than not, one member of the group would sneak out to take a call or return an e-mail—even if the meeting was at an important juncture.

We say fourteen pairs of eyes and not fifteen because one of the managers knew that the call could not be for him. He had a cell phone, but he had turned it off for the duration of the meeting. He still used a paper calendar (gasp!), and he did not own a BlackBerry, a device that was ubiquitous in the firm. (For the uninitiated, a BlackBerry is a brand of PDA that makes it easy to receive and reply to e-mails on the go.) During the course of the meeting, the subject of BlackBerries came up.

"I couldn't live without mine," offered one participant.

"Yes," agreed another, "it's my lifeline. I'm never out of touch."

Praise for the device was universal. Except for our young manager, Ben.

"I don't even own a BlackBerry," Ben announced calmly.

The others in the room looked at him in amazement. Why in the world not, they asked. How could he possibly live without one?

"I just don't feel the need for it," Ben replied. "I'll check my e-mail when I get back to the office. My assistant knows to call me in case of a true emergency."

This was a fairly genial group of people, and they began to joke with Ben about his apparent lack of efficiency.

Unfazed, Ben said, "Seriously, I don't need to run around like a chicken with my head cut off. My stuff gets done. And my region does at least as much business as any of yours." That quieted the room. The interesting thing was that in our opinion (based on more than just this short interaction), Ben was probably the highest-potential manager there, despite being the youngest. We could envision him as a top executive someday; many of the others, we suspected, had probably reached the highest level they ever would.[14]

Our point is not that the use of BlackBerries limits one's career track, or that the use of a paper calendar is somehow superior to the use of a PDA. (In fact, one of us—who will for now remain nameless—is a confirmed gadget freak, having cycled through ten laptops as well as various Palm Pilots, Pocket PCs, and two *truly* geeky handheld PCs.)

But technology or no technology, if we allow ourselves to become slaves to *chronos*, then we have to ask ourselves whether we still have our eyes on the prize. Time masters never forget that there is a difference between *efficiency* and *effectiveness*. Efficiency has to do with minimizing waste, finding ways to do things faster and incrementally better. Effectiveness, on the other hand, has to do with doing the right things in the first place. You could be the world's most efficient manufacturer of eight-track tapes today, but how effective would that be?

Truly effective leadership depends upon a synthesis of both views of time. Effective leaders must first be superb time managers. They must, among myriad other things, meet deadlines, schedule events, and worry about time to market. But they must also go on to see and exploit the kairotic windows of opportunity that, for example, come immediately after a technological innovation. They frequently grant their team members the freedom to take control and to move at their own pace, without interference. If a team is in the zone, they often lead by *not* leading. They realize that things do not always have to be done by the clock.

They know that although temporal intelligence is partly innate, it can be, like a pure golf swing or a complex arpeggio, continuously improved.

They supplement *chronos*—the analytical, sequential, and rational capacities of the brain's left hemisphere—with *kairos*—the creative and immensely powerful capacities of the right hemisphere.

■ HOW YOU CAN APPLY TEMPORAL INTELLIGENCE

Time masters know that effective leaders must first be superb time managers. But they also know that the real power comes from kairotic time. As you try to balance *chronos* and *kairos*, keep in mind that:

- ■ Timing is everything. Do the right thing at the right time. Discern the *when* as well as the *what*. Recognize opportunity and seize it before it is lost. Become astutely aware of opportunities that might not recur and auspicious moments of decision, and find the precisely right time to act. Your sense of timing is fundamental to leadership, and acting prematurely can be as deadly to the success of an initiative as tardiness.

- ■ You must look for the turning points. Time masters constantly scan the temporal horizon, searching for those decisive moments and pivotal convergences that have the capacity to change everything. Once you sense the presence of one of these rare kairotic moments, get everyone focused on the task at hand.

- ■ Like Andy Grove, you should sometimes take yourself out of time. Ask yourself, "If I were just hired today, would I choose the same strategy that we have now?" This ability to place yourself in a new temporal context can provide stunning clarity in difficult situations.

- ■ Grant team members the freedom to take control and to move at their own pace. Resist the tempta-

tion to interfere. Lead, at times, by not leading. Realize that there is often no need to increase the
team's sense of urgency, no imperative to insist
that things be done by the clock, no necessity to
insist upon due dates. You'll have your team so in
the zone that its members have assumed a "total
commitment" philosophy. Don't disrupt this kairotic process.

CHAPTER 6

TIME AS ENERGIZER

LIKE ALL ORGANIC SYSTEMS, companies (and industries) seem naturally to age and to ossify. A once proud and energetic culture loses its vitality. A market is saturated or, worse, becomes stagnant and declines. A highly profitable specialty product degenerates into a mere commodity. As the life cycle progresses, so do enterprises and economic sectors. Companies and industries are born, grow, mature, and die. The sigmoid curve—that fascinating S-shape—insists that in everything we start slowly, then experiment and falter, then grow rapidly, then wax, then wane. Its whiplike curves model everything from the product life cycle to the trajectory of human life.

As this inexorable temporal arc rises and falls, it is the manager's job to battle the inevitable: to prolong the growth cycle, discern the onset of maturity, and prevent decline. It's quite a ride. The growth phase is usually exhilaratingly entrepreneurial, the maturity phase highly profitable, and the decline phase downright depressing—with the grim reaper punctuating the sigmoid curve's awful finality.

Sometimes an entire industry goes into decline. Consider, for example, the airlines. The last few years have been dismal for this embattled sector, with annual losses approximating $15 billion. In an industry that is not known for profits (it has lost more money than it has made since the advent of flight in 1903), high labor costs, the growing overcapacity, the aggressive cost cutting, the sweeping impact of Internet-based ticketing, and the challenge of cut-rate carriers have created the worst crisis in its history. With terminally sick balance sheets (typical debt-to-equity ratios are skyrocketing to 90 percent), major carriers are facing bankruptcy and liquidation. Add the Iraq war, with its pressure on fuel prices and passenger revenue, and you have the makings of a historic industrywide crash.

Is this economic necessity or just the ravages of time?

▌ HELL IN A HANDBASKET

It could be both. For centuries, science has joined with legend to perpetuate the idea that the passage of time generally spoils things. Nowhere is this truer than in the second law of thermodynamics, postulated in 1850 by scientists who noticed that no machine ever yields as much energy as it consumes. Hence, whenever work is done, some amount of usable energy is lost.

The second law threatened the timelessness implied by Newton's mechanistic model of the universe. Energy, a group of German scientists discovered, flows from greater concentration to greater diffusion or dispersal. A pot of boiling water, for example, cools down when it is taken off the stove. Its thermal energy flows out into the cooler kitchen air. At a more cosmic level, the second law posited that the universe was essentially a giant heat pump that is slowly running out of fuel. This process could be measured by *entropy*, a quantity that expands as energy dissipates. Simply put, entropy is the amount of disorder a system contains.

Time's arrow, it seemed, pointed in only one direction—toward bedlam and decay. A cup of coffee grows cold; Humpty Dumpty falls off the wall. Things go to hell.

■ TIME MANAGEMENT

When such chaos threatens organizations, managers—understandably—seek to turn things around with definitive action. They hunker down. They focus on those things that they can control. They create more structure, begin to micromanage, emphasize efficiency over effectiveness, and encourage following rather than leading. They downsize, consolidate, restructure. They manage.

Time becomes a negative force. Consider, for example, the opening scene of the film *Cast Away*, where Tom Hanks's character, manager Chuck Noland, is in Moscow training a number of Russian FedEx employees. By FedEx standards, the performance of the Moscow office has been dismal, and Noland is there to change that.

"Time rules over us without mercy," he bellows, his words roughly translated by an assistant, "not caring if we're healthy or ill, hungry or drunk, Russian or American or beings from Mars. It's like a fire: It can either destroy us or keep us warm. That's why every FedEx office has a clock. Because we live or we die by the clock. We never turn our back on it. And we never ever allow ourselves the *sin* of losing track of time!"

A young boy then brings Noland a tube-shaped FedEx package. Noland has clearly been expecting it. He explains that he mailed the package to himself before leaving the United States for Russia. "I wonder what it could be," he asks rhetorically while opening the package. "Architectural plans? Technical drawings? New wallpaper for the bathroom?" He then reveals its contents: a digital timer, still running. He stops it at 87 hours, 22 minutes, 17 seconds—the precise length of time it took for the package to get from Memphis, Tennessee, to its destination in Moscow.

Noland is incensed. "Eighty-seven hours is a shameful outrage!" he tells his audience. "Eighty-seven hours is an eternity. The cosmos was created in less time! Wars have been fought and nations toppled in eighty-seven hours! Fortunes made and squandered!"

Time is the enemy, and we aren't about to go down without a fight.

▌ WHEN TIME IS *NOT* MONEY

Many of us, in our time management–obsessed world, are like Noland. Rarely do we think of time as a positive force.

There are exceptions, of course. We recently explained the magical concept of compound annual growth to a twelve-year-old. "You mean you just put money in the bank, and it grows?" he asked in amazement. "Sweet!" Sometimes, time is indeed money.

Yet we tend to think about time and money in very different, and revealing, ways. Hong Kong University of Science and Technology researcher Dilap Soman has studied the relationship between time and money, and the ways in which we account for them. His findings reveal much about the ways in which we value—or fail to value—time.

Soman's research involves the concept of sunk costs, something that is most commonly applied to financial situations. A classic example of a sunk cost involves tickets to a basketball game. Say that Fred pays $50 for a ticket to Friday's game. Barney is luckier: He gets a free ticket for being employee of the month at the quarry. When Friday arrives, though, so does a snowstorm. Neither man likes driving in the snow. Are they equally likely to go, despite the weather?

According to economic theory, they should be. What matters are the marginal costs and benefits to be realized *from this point in time onward.* Past expenditures should not enter into the equation. The fact that Fred paid for his ticket in the past and Barney got his for free in the past should be irrelevant to the current decision.

Yet research confirms what most people would probably guess: Fred is much more likely to go to the game than Barney is. The most reasonable explanation is this: When he bought his ticket, Fred opened a mental account that we'll call "basketball." That account started with a deficit of $50. His original plan was to realize at least $50 worth of benefit, in the form of enjoyment, upon attending the game. If he fails to attend the game, however, he will have to close out that account with a $50 loss. Most of us don't like to do that. Barney's mental basketball account, on the other hand, has a zero balance, so he is content to close it out without attending the game.

You might think that people would be more logical when they are dealing with the company's money. But you'd be wrong. One of us used to be an analyst for an American company that wanted to build power plants in developing nations. The firm was considering a plant in Pakistan (hey, it seemed like a good idea at the time). We invested more than $10 million in up-front costs for surveys, licenses, and the like. Then, for various reasons, we began to sour on the deal. Our in-country partner started to make us nervous. The financial projections were revised downward. We couldn't get political risk insurance for the project. It became pretty clear that we should not build the plant.

Still, that $10 million loomed large in our minds. Otherwise rational executives were caught in the sunk cost trap: "We've already spent millions of dollars—we can't just walk away with nothing!" Of course, the right decision was indeed to walk away, since we believed that staying would mean even larger losses. Ultimately, cooler heads prevailed. But some companies waste millions, even billions of dollars chasing sunk costs.

Soman's question was an intriguing one: Do people think about sunk *time* costs in the same way they think about sunk financial costs?

To find an answer, he conducted a series of controlled experiments. In one, he presented respondents with scenarios similar to our Fred and Barney example. Essentially, Soman asked undergraduate students to imagine that they have paid $60 for a theater ticket and $20 for a rock concert ticket, both nonrefundable. They later realize that both performances are on the same night—it will be impossible for them to attend both. They must choose one. Significantly, Soman tells students that they expect to enjoy the rock concert more than the theatrical performance.

Which did they choose? Nearly 62 percent chose the theatrical performance, even though they expected to enjoy it less! This is quite irrational. The sunk cost of $60 should be irrelevant—it's gone forever, and it can't be regained no matter what happens now—but people simply can't help themselves. They want to avoid the larger perceived "loss" associated with giving up the theater ticket.

Here's the interesting part. Soman presented another group of students with a similar scenario, except that here, they have spent fifteen hours working as a research assistant in exchange for the theater ticket, and only five hours in exchange for the rock concert ticket. The sunk cost is expressed in time, rather than money. Because the differential is the same—the theater ticket is still three times as "expensive" as the rock concert ticket—it would stand to reason that when forced to choose, around 62 percent of students would choose to attend the theater.

But they didn't. In fact, only 5 percent chose to attend the theater, while 95 percent picked the rock concert! For some reason, there appears to be very little sunk cost effect when temporal investments are considered. On the surface, this sounds like a good thing; after all, considering sunk costs is irrational. If people ignore sunk time costs, what's wrong with that?

Not quite sure what to make of these results, however, Soman developed two hypotheses. One possibility, he suggested, is that people are in fact more rational when considering time than they are when considering money. On the other hand, perhaps people are somehow unable or unwilling to account for temporal investments; they either can't or don't value time the way they do money.

After performing a number of additional experiments, Soman concluded what common sense would suggest: "This lack of attention to sunk costs was not due to increased rationality but rather to difficulties in mentally accounting for time."[1] Apparently we find it so difficult to quantify the value of time that we don't bother.

Yet time is much, much more valuable than money—it's the one resource that we can't create, copy, or stockpile. And while we should not consider *sunk* time costs, we should start to view time itself as a resource, an ally—not something that always drains or enervates, but something that can *energize*.

■ OPEN SYSTEMS

Indeed, time is not merely something to be endured, dealt with, or *managed.* This refreshing thought is largely the product of three remarkable men: British naturalist Charles Darwin, French philosopher and Nobel Prize winner Henri Bergson, and fellow Nobel laureate and chemist Ilya Prigogine.

Darwin's discovery of biological evolution—and with it the ground-breaking idea that things might actually improve over time—transformed the gloom and doom of the second law and entropy into optimism about the future. The cosmic machine might be running out of fuel, but biological systems are endlessly energetic as time passes and (of even greater importance) seem to be becoming *more*, not less, organized. Thanks to Darwin, the effect of time's passage suddenly was seen in a new and positive light.

Time's arrow now seemed pointed toward order and progress, and away from chaos and degeneration.

The iconoclastic and cultish Bergson, whose lectures at the Collège de France were so popular that students called the school "the house of Bergson," added fuel to Darwin's fire. Bergson's original thinking (he argued that intuition often goes deeper than the intellect and rejected Newton's mechanistic view of nature) not only got his books black-listed by the Catholic church but also inspired Marcel Proust's great novel, *In Search of Lost Time* (sometimes translated as *Remembrance of Things Past*).

Bergson believed that time's passage did not enervate, as the second law had insisted. Instead, it energized. To Bergson, time's passage was the source of all creative impulse, the wellspring of "living energy." As he put it in *Time and Free Will*, time "is a perpetual recreation of the self and sustained becoming that cannot be halted or isolated." Time, he proclaimed, was the "very medium of innovation."[2]

More recently, the late chemist Ilya Prigogine built on the foundation of Darwin and Bergson, postulating new ways of thinking about time. As one interviewer put it, "To Prigogine, time is the forgotten dimension. His lifelong efforts have been directed toward better understanding its role in the universe."[3] Prigogine was a man of encyclopedic learning who devoured the classics and could read piano scores before he could read words. Throughout his working life, he divided his time between Brussels and his Center for Statistical Mechanics and Thermodynamics at the University of Texas.

He sensed what others had missed: that the second law of thermodynamics and its corollary, entropy, assume a *closed* system, a kind of perpetual-motion machine isolated from the rest of the world. Of course neither living things nor the Earth is walled off from the rest of the universe. They coexist in open systems, inescapable networks of information and feedback that humans in particular—the most adaptive and inquisitive of species—find essential to their survival and success.

In an interview, Prigogine explained closed versus open systems using an analogy about two towns. One, he said, is walled off from the outside world; the other is a nexus of commerce. The first town represents the closed system of classical physics and chemistry, which must decay according to the second law of thermodynamics. The second town is able to grow and become more complex because of its interactions with the surrounding environment.

The point is that when survival and success are threatened, healthy systems that lose their equilibrium can evolve into (as Prigogine put it) "dissipative structures," regrouping in preparation to move in new directions. Disequilibrium, not equilibrium, and complexity, not simplicity, are the precursors to real growth and regeneration. They are requisite conditions for future health and robustness. Prigogine's idea gave birth to the notion that exhausted organizations—dissipative structures—possess the capacity to experience a rebirth, to "self-organize" over time.

■ CHAOS THEORY, FIREFLIES, AND ECONOMICS

This concept of self-organization—one of the major branches of what's now called chaos theory—gets even more interesting when we consider, of all things, fireflies.

Surely one of the joys of summer is the reappearance of the firefly—or the lightning bug, as some of us call it. What child has not chased after these marvels of nature, perhaps trying to catch enough in a jar to make a natural lantern? It's a rite of summer. The difficulty (and the fun) is actually catching one. You never know quite where the bug will fly, or when it will emit its tantalizing light. There seems to be no discernible pattern, no predictability.

But that's not true of all fireflies. Travel to Thailand, for instance, and you can observe one of nature's most remarkable sights. There the fireflies pulse *in unison*. And not just two or three fireflies next to each other. You might see thousands, even millions of fireflies pulsing as one, flashing every three seconds or so. Travel down a river outside Bangkok, and you might see mile after mile of synchronized fireflies on the banks.

Residents of Asia and certain parts of Africa have observed this amazing display since the dawn of mankind, but it wasn't until the early twentieth century that the phenomenon caught the attention of Western scientists. It became a scientific mystery. The journal *Science* alone published more than twenty articles on the phenomenon between 1915 and 1935, with a variety of explanations. One scientist attributed the synchronous light display to an optical illusion, caused by the blinking of his own eyes. Others suggested that some odd atmospheric condition was causing a common physical reaction in the insects.

Some believed that there must be a head firefly, a "maestro" who somehow signaled the others. "If it is desired to get a body of men to sing or play together in perfect rhythm they not only must have a leader but must be trained to follow such a leader," wrote George Hudson in 1918. "Do these insects inherit a sense of rhythm more perfect than our own?"[4] Of course not. Such a thought was absurd. Or was it?

The answer remained a mystery until the 1960s, when bi-
ologist John Buck traveled to Thailand and performed an impromptu experiment. He and his wife caught a few dozen
Asian fireflies and set them loose in their dark hotel room. At
first the insects flew about and flashed randomly. Eventually,
though, they settled down, and pairs of fireflies began to
pulse in unison, then trios, then larger groups. Buck hypothesized that there wasn't any maestro firefly; somehow all of
the insects were adjusting to the other fireflies around them.
In addition, he guessed, they must have some sort of internal
metronome, or clock, that paced the flashes at three-second
intervals. There is no record of what the hotel staff thought
of this experiment.

Subsequent experiments confirmed the idea that the
fireflies synchronize to one another without any overarching,
conscious direction. They simply synchronize with the fireflies nearest to them, creating small pods of synchrony that,
in turn, synchronize with one another, until eventually all are
glowing in harmony. In fact, if you think about it, how *could*
there be a single maestro? If there can be a two-mile-long
chain of synchronized fireflies along a winding river (and
there can), how in the world could the maestro signal the
insects a mile up the river, around the bend? Those faraway
insects could not possibly see the maestro, or smell his pher-
omones, or hear his call, quickly enough to achieve perfect
synchrony. The best possible result would be some sort of
cascading effect, like "the wave" in a football stadium. But
the fireflies achieve a state of stunning unison.

Today, science accepts as obvious the once-controversial
idea that complex systems, like fireflies, can organize themselves without conscious direction. Steven Strogatz's fascinating 2003 book *Sync: The Emerging Science of Spontaneous*

Order contains numerous examples, from biology to astrophysics. As we discussed in Chapter 4, the process by which various individual rhythms fall into sync is called *entrainment*, a concept fundamental to temporal intelligence and the capacity to self-organize.

Now, though, let's consider the *self-organizing* nature of the fireflies. In his *Science* article back in 1918, George Hudson contended that to get men to play perfectly together, they "not only must have a leader but must be trained to follow such a leader."[5] Is that true? Today, it probably isn't very controversial to answer no. To stick with Hudson's own musical analogy, what about jazz? While one member of a jazz group *may* serve as maestro, that isn't always so. Often, leaderless jazz musicians are seamlessly synchronizing with each other, speeding up or slowing down in what sounds, to our ears, like spontaneous order. (In fairness to Mr. Hudson, he was writing before jazz became popular; big songs in 1918 included the rather un-jazzy "Till We Meet Again" and "Beautiful Ohio.")

In fact, our entire economy is an example of a complex self-organized system. Back in 1776, Adam Smith posited that individuals acting in their own self-interest, under certain conditions and without central coordination, could achieve spontaneous order as if guided by some invisible hand.

It seems that he was right. Have you ever been in a movie theater and wanted some popcorn? Think about it: How did that popcorn get there? Is there some centralized Popcorn Command Center running analyses on a supercomputer, predicting that someone would need one medium tub of popcorn at precisely this point in time during the showing of this particular movie? Of course not. It was simply in the self-interest of someone to get popcorn to you. No one told popcorn makers to do it. But the demand for movie popcorn exists, and smart people notice that demand and find ways to satisfy it.

Yet plenty of smart, well-meaning people have tried to plan economies at amazingly precise levels of detail. Consider the five-year economic plans of the former Soviet Union. Essentially, a group of economists would decide, say, how many dump trucks would be needed in Latvia in five years. Then they would work backwards, deciding how much steel would be needed for that many trucks, and then how much iron ore and manganese would need to be mined to supply the steel mills, and then . . . you get the idea. The calculations for dump trucks alone were incredibly complex, not to mention insensitive—they had no way to allow for any changes in the economic environment over the next five years. It simply couldn't be done, which is why the Soviets often ran out of things like toilet paper, and why we now speak of the *former* Soviet Union.

By contrast, the capitalist system seems chaotic. No centralized body decides what the supply of any given product should be. No one is minding the store. Yet somehow the system *self-organizes* over time. When was the last time you wanted to buy popcorn, but couldn't? Or toilet paper? Or a dump truck, for that matter? Somehow, our needs are met quite well in the almost complete absence of master planning. Given certain premises—that people tend to act in their own self-interest, that they will benefit from their own labor and innovation, that those who don't play fair will be punished—over time spontaneous order succeeds where central planning could not. With extremely complex systems like economies, in fact, self-organization may be the only choice.[6]

In organizational design, we attempt to impose order upon chaos. Structure is comforting. It seems like the safe and logical thing to do. We recently saw the organizational chart for a large electronics manufacturer, run by people who started out as electrical engineers. It filled a poster-sized sheet of paper, using small print, boxes, and arrows. From the back of the room, it looked just like a drawing of a complex electric circuit. Frederick Taylor, the father of scientific management, would be proud.

With our detailed organizational matrices and master plans, we attempt to seal off the system so that outside forces don't screw things up, and so that energy doesn't escape. Yet this is rather like taping up all of the windows and doors in your house—it sounds like a good idea, but if you close up your house too tightly, no fresh air gets in. Margaret Wheatley, in her book *Leadership and the New Science*, puts it this way: "It is both sad and ironic that we have treated organizations like machines, acting as though they were dead when all this time they've been living, open systems capable of self renewal."

An *open system* interacts with its environment, adapting and evolving over time. According to Wheatley, open systems "don't sit quietly by as their energy dissipates. They don't seek equilibrium. Quite the opposite. To stay viable, open systems maintain a state of non-equilibrium, keeping the system off balance so that it can change and grow."[7] Successful open systems are not stable, but *resilient over time*. This was at the heart of Prigogine's research, for which he won the Nobel Prize in 1977.

■ THE VIRTUE OF DOING NOTHING

If we take only a snapshot view of a system or an organization, we can't necessarily tell whether evolution is taking place. After all, Prigogine discovered his self-organizing structures only by introducing the element of *time* into his experiments. Leaders, too, must let time have its way.

In January 2001, for example, midway through the National Hockey League season, John Tortorella became head coach of the Tampa Bay Lightning. It was a young franchise, in existence for only nine years, and it was performing poorly. The team had never won a playoff series. By the end of the 2000–2001 season, the team had won just twenty-four of its eighty-four games. Few observers blamed Tortorella for this poor showing; after all, he had taken over in midseason, a difficult task under any circumstances. Going forward, he was to be the solution to the team's problems.

During the following season, though, the team won just twenty-seven games, a minimal improvement at best. The anticipated turnaround did not seem to be occurring. It didn't take long for fans to call for the heads of Tortorella and the new general manager, Jay Feaster, who obviously knew little about running a successful hockey team. Radio talk shows simmered with indignation. Everyone, including the team's previous general manager, was calling for trades of young, underperforming players. Yet Tortorella and Feaster were apparently oblivious. Where were the blockbuster trades? Where was the bias for action?

Then something strange happened: The Lightning started to win. During the 2002–2003 season, the Lightning won thirty-six games. Goalie Nikolai Khabibulin was stopping so many goals that fans took to calling him "the Bulin Wall." In the postseason, the team defeated the Washington Capitals— the first playoff series win in the franchise's history.

Continuing the momentum from the previous year, the 2003–2004 season started quite well, and despite a midseason slump, the team leaders made no significant changes. The team ended up winning forty-six games and the Eastern Conference regular-season championship. Martin St. Louis, a relatively young player, scored more points that season than any other player in the National Hockey League.

In the postseason playoffs, the Lightning defeated the New York Islanders, the Montreal Canadiens, and the Philadelphia Flyers, making it to their first Stanley Cup finals, where they faced the Calgary Flames. It was a difficult series, going a full seven games. Game 7 was close, too, decided by a thin 2–1 score. In the end, though, Tampa Bay triumphed.

Forty-year-old veteran Dave Andreychuk was finally able to skate around the rink holding the Stanley Cup high above his head. Team owner William Davidson, whose Detroit Pistons had won the National Basketball Association championship just a few weeks before, became the first owner to simultaneously hold championship trophies from two major sports leagues.

But the intriguing thing is how the Lightning got to that point. How did Tortorella and Feaster take a group of primarily young, inconsistent players and turn them into a championship team?

Goalie Khabibulin told the Associated Press what he thought was the secret of the team's success: "Doing nothing."[8]

As Khabibulin explained, the team's leaders believed in the group of players they had assembled and recognized their innate promise. Even in the face of significant—and very public—pressure, they refused to make changes for the sake of change. They understood that some strategies take time to develop. For them, time was not an enemy, draining the energy from the organization, but an ally.

We're guessing that Tortorella didn't describe the Lightning as a dissipative structure in many team meetings. It's also quite possible that he does *not* have a picture of Ilya Prigogine on his office wall. Yet in the face of seeming chaos and disorder, the team somehow experienced a rebirth, a self-organization. And it was patience, not swift action, that allowed the improvement.

This is a lesson that is understood by one of the most successful women in the world: Oprah Winfrey. The first African American woman to become a billionaire, Winfrey was named one of the most influential people of the twentieth century by *Time* in 1998. *The Oprah Winfrey Show* has become a cultural touchstone; even U.S. presidents show up as guests. Books touted in Oprah's on-air book club become instant best-sellers. She owns a major production company, Harpo Productions. Somehow, she also found time to earn an Oscar nomination for best supporting actress in *The Color Purple.*

Surely this is a woman of action. Yet, she told an interviewer in 1991, one of the secrets of her success is sometimes *not* acting:

> One of the biggest lessons I've learned recently is that when you don't know what to do, you should do nothing until you figure out what to do because a lot of times you feel like you are pressed against the wall, and you've got to make a decision.
>
> You never have to do anything. Don't know what to do? Do nothing. I wait. And that has been a big lesson: to be willing, to be still with myself, and trust myself and my higher power to help me make the right decision. And to not feel pressured.[9]

When things are going wrong in an organization, our natural inclination is to take control, to seek equilibrium, to impose order on chaos. The bigger the problem, the bigger the required action. Yet as we have seen, often the best decision is no decision.

It takes a good deal of temporal intelligence to know when to act and when to let time work its magic. Our point is certainly not to advocate inaction over action in every instance, or even in most. Taken to its extreme, this would be little more than an excuse for entrenched management, a justification for laziness. But sometimes, making a decision is actually the easy way out. In a culture with an overwhelming bias toward action, perhaps it makes sense to remind ourselves that time can indeed heal some wounds.

■ AN ANGEL IN THE ROOM

"The notes I handle no better than many pianists," Arthur Schnabel once said. "But the pauses between the notes—ah, that is where the art resides!"[10] The famed concert pianist obviously possessed a virtuoso's refined sense of the sound, and the energizing potential, of silence.

One of us experienced the power of such "white spaces" (as Liz Claiborne's Paul Charron calls them) while summering in the beautiful Burgundian town of Chalon-sur-Saône. We'd been invited to dinner by a French couple who wanted us to see what France was *really* like." Their home turned out to be a charming country house surrounded by vineyards. After the *grandpère* presided over a tour of the winery grounds and offered endless samples of the family wines, we settled in for dinner—at around nine o'clock—with several other guests.

The menu was spectacular. Snails wrapped in puff pastry topped with a bleu cheese sauce. Lamb chops encrusted with fresh herbs. Classic onion soup. French cuisine and wine at their very best. The conversation was lilting and sometimes hilarious—made even more so by our efforts to demonstrate our prowess with the French language.

Time seemed to have simply stopped on that exquisite July evening. Suddenly it was nearly midnight, and as dessert and coffee complemented the talk around the table, our host played selections from his record library of classic American jazz. In this marvelous time warp, we were listening to Louis Armstrong, "King" Oliver, Jelly Roll Martin, Charlie Parker, Chuck Mangione.

For most of the evening, the conversation flowed freely. And then something happened that we will never forget. For several minutes, no one said a word. Except for the soft strains of jazz, there was absolute silence. To the Americans in the room, this was extremely uncomfortable. Had the evening died?

After a few minutes of this silence, however, our hostess said something fascinating. "Isn't that beautiful," she said. "An angel just flew through the room." For her, the quiet moment was not awkward, but touching, even profound.

Only then did we fully appreciate the temporal gift we had been given on that unforgettable evening in Burgundy: the "white space" that Schnabel and Charron so deeply treasured.

It's easy to get caught in the temporal gears of daily life. Constantly checking off items on our to-do lists, racing from meeting to meeting, checking our e-mail, we tend to forget that it's generally our "down time" that allows deep thought, creativity, and innovation to occur. Like most of us, time masters are always interested in ways to do more in a day. But they also understand that sometimes it's even more important to do less.

They appreciate the spaces in between the notes.

∎ SEEDING THE FUTURE

Farmers and gardeners intuitively understand the energizing power of time. After all, every spring they plant seeds—and then wait. Time is not the enemy here; farmers do not fret that time is "wasting away," as so many of us do. Instead, time is an ally, a positive force. Each day during the growing season brings the farmer closer to reward; when enough time has passed, he will literally reap the harvest. It's a ridiculously simple idea, so simple that we tend to miss its significance. Yet the metaphor of planting seeds is a useful way to think about time in other aspects of life.

On a personal level, consider the job search as an example. Every résumé you send out, every phone call you make, every job-related conversation is a seed. Once sent, a batch of résumés is out there in the world, working for you; over time, something good *can* happen to you. That doesn't necessarily mean that something good *will* happen, of course. After all, other factors—the job market, your experience, those typos you missed in your cover letter—have something to do with success. But now, at least, time is working for you. Plant enough high-quality seeds and something is bound to grow.

Aspiring writers are well advised to always have something they have written under consideration by a potential publisher. As long as your work is being read, your chance for success is alive. The phone could ring at any moment. If you have no manuscripts out in the world working for you, then by definition nothing positive can happen, and (perhaps this is the key psychological insight) you are much more likely to become frustrated, to give up. As a lottery commercial once put it, "You gotta be in it to win it." When you send out those manuscripts, you are sowing hope.

Leaders with a high level of temporal intelligence understand that this dynamic also exists at the organizational level. Like individuals, groups can benefit from the potential energy of time. What might this look like? For a consulting firm, it might take the form of proposals submitted or bids on potential projects. For a manufacturing firm, it might be that exciting stable of new products in the pipeline. For a retail chain, it might be a bold new marketing campaign whose results are eagerly anticipated. In all of these situations, time is a positive force. The seeds have been planted, and we are eagerly awaiting their growth. Rather than cursing time for taking something away from us, we are looking with anticipation to the future.

The key is not just to do these things—as competent professionals, you are already planting such seeds in the normal course of business. The key is to appreciate their temporal dimension. Quite simply, hope is motivating. And what is hope if not time-based—a vision of what the future may be?

Whatever the nature of your business and its typical cycles or rhythms, regularly ask yourself how many seeds you currently have germinating. What is in development, in process? If you and your people believe that today there is some chance—no matter how remote—that the phone may ring with great news, then time is working for you, not against you. If, on the other hand, you are constantly dreading each day, searching for ways to cram a few more hours into the week, then you are still viewing time negatively.

Plant some seeds, and see what grows in this climate.

■ HOW YOU CAN APPLY TEMPORAL INTELLIGENCE

People tend to think of time as an obstacle to be overcome, endured, managed. But it's much more than that. Here are some ways to profit from the *energizing* nature of time:

- Allow time for teams to self-organize. Effective organizations are often like jazz groups, with the players adjusting to one another in a complex, and seemingly chaotic, process. The key insight, for time masters, is that this process does not always benefit from centralized control. If a team's melody isn't immediately apparent, sometimes all the team needs is time.

- Decide not to decide. There are times when the best thing to do is nothing. Some problems will disappear. Others will solve themselves. Still others will benefit from new information and perspectives.

- Create white space and cherish it. Constant activity doesn't always lead to productivity. Without reflection, people are little different from ants. Stop scurrying around and take time to think.

■ Always have something in the pipeline. If every time the phone rings, you believe that it *could* herald great news, then time is an energizing force for you. If you lack that feeling, or even dread the phone's ring, then you should plant more organizational seeds.

EPILOGUE

IN WRITING THIS BOOK, we have taken a journey through time, a vast subject that is greatly misunderstood. Probing this most universal yet most mysterious of subjects has been a challenging quest, giving us a new respect for St. Augustine's lament in his *Confessions*, "What then, is time? If no one asks me, I know. If I wish to explain it to someone who asks, I know it not."

Yet five years of research, much of it gleaned from the narratives of corporate leaders so temporally savvy that we began calling them "time masters," have convinced us that *time*'s time has come, that temporal intelligence can significantly improve leaders' effectiveness by enhancing their awareness and knowledge of time.

We believe that temporal intelligence is as important to leadership success as long-heralded behaviors such as empowering others, modeling the way, challenging the status quo, and creating shared visions. Whether it is a fresh, new sense of how a team's rhythm can be discerned and then changed, or of how slicing, dicing, and calendarizing time can be trumped by the continuous flow of peak experience, time's fascinating intersection with almost everything that leaders do is ubiquitous.

For these reasons, we are convinced that time and timing are essential inputs that determine the success or failure of everything from organization change efforts to breaking into new markets successfully. This uniquely human force (one that has encouraged permanence, constancy, and equilibrium for mankind since the dawn of history) also carries in its relentless DNA the power to drive radical change and transformation.

We hope that this book is a call to action, one that has awakened new interest in expanding the breadth of your temporal repertoire. That you now possess the ability to see time through many different lenses. And that you, like our time masters, will begin your own quest—a journey that will enable you to truly understand time, not just measure it by a clock.

Like our journey, yours will not be an easy passage. "For tribal man space was the uncontrollable mystery," warned Marshall McLuhan in *The Mechanical Bride*. "For technological man it is time that occupies the same role."

But we believe that this exciting new adventure will be worth the effort, and that enhancing your temporal intelligence will help you to harness this remarkable source of leadership energy.

NOTES

INTRODUCTION

1. As quoted in Marilyn Norris, "Warren Bennis on Rebuilding Leadership," *Planning Review,* September 1, 1992.

CHAPTER 1

1. Po Bronson, "The Long Now," *Wired* 6, no. 5 (1998): 116–139.
2. Stewart Brand, "Taking the Long View," *Time* 155, no. 17 (2000): 86; and Stewart Brand, "The Long Now Foundation: Goals," www.longnow.org/about/about.htm, accessed February 13, 2004.
3. Brand, "Taking the Long View."
4. Tony Kornheiser, "Question with Authority," *Washington Post,* February 26, 2004, D1.
5. Constance Holden, "Your Words Betray You," *Science* 300, no. 5619 (April 25, 2003): 577.
6. Quoted in Albert R. Hunt, "The U.N. to Bush's Rescue?" *Wall Street Journal,* April 22, 2004, A19.
7. Alexander Keyssar and Ernest May, "Education for Public Service in the United States: A History," in *For the People: Can We*

Fix Public Service? ed. John D. Donahue and Joseph S. Nye, Jr. (Washington, D.C.: Brookings Institution, 2003), 101.

8. Matea Gold. "The Race to the White House: Dean Campaigns in the Past Tense," *Los Angeles Times*, February 17, 2004, A15.

9. Patrick O'Brian, *Post Captain* (New York: Norton, 1972), 99.

10. James G. March, "Exploration and Exploitation in Organizational Learning," *Organization Science* 2 (1991): 71–87.

11. Jim Collins, "Leadership Lessons of a Rock Climber," *Fast Company*, no. 77 (2003): 109–110.

12. See Janet Lowe, *Jack Welch Speaks: Wisdom from the World's Greatest Business Leader* (New York: John Wiley & Sons, 2001); James W. Robinson, *Jack Welch on Leadership: Executive Lessons From the Master CEO* (New York: Precidio, 2001); Robert Slater, *Jack Welch and the GE Way: Management Insights and Leadership Secrets of the Legendary CEO* (New York: McGraw-Hill, 1998).

13. Jerry Useem, "Another Boss Another Revolution," *Fortune* 149, no. 7 (2004): 124.

14. Joanne Bischmann, quoted in Danielle Sacks, "Fast Talk: Brands We Love," *Fast Company*, no. 85 (2004): 44.

CHAPTER 2

1. Allen C. Bluedorn, *The Human Organization of Time: Temporal Realities and Experience* (Stanford, Calif.: Stanford Business Books, 2002), 50.

2. Jared Sandberg, "To-Do Lists Can Take More Time Than Doing, but That Isn't the Point," *Wall Street Journal*, September 8, 2004, B1.

3. Ian Parker, "Absolute PowerPoint: The Annals of Business," *New Yorker* 77, no. 13 (2001): 76.

4. Ibid., 87.

5. Teresa M. Amabile, Constance N. Hadley, and Steven J. Kramer, "Creativity Under the Gun," *Harvard Business Review* 80, no. 8 (2002): 52.

6. "The Fifteen Questions by Eli Siegel," reprinted in *Journal of Aesthetics & Art Criticism* (December 1955).

7. David Hajdu, "Wynton's Blues," *Atlantic Monthly* 291, no. 2 (2003): 44.

8. Ronald E. Purser and Jack Petranker, "Unfreezing the Future: Utilizing Dynamic Time for Deep Improvisation in Organizational Change," paper presented at the Dynamic Time and Creative Inquiry in Organizational Change Conference, Boston, Mass., June 18–21, 2002.

9. Gerda Reith, review of *The Risk Society and Beyond: Critical Issues for Social Theory,* by Barbara Adam, Ulrich Beck, and Joost van Loon (eds.), *Time & Society* 11, no. 1 (2002): 157–158.

10. Manuel Schneider, "Time at High Altitude: Experiencing Time on the Roof of the World," *Time & Society* 11, no. 1 (2002): 145–146.

11. Mihaly Csikszentmihalyi, *Good Business: Leadership, Flow, and the Making of Meaning* (New York: Viking Penguin, 2003), 64.

12. Keith H. Hammonds, "Michael Porter's Big Ideas," *Fast Company*, no. 44 (2001): 150.

13. Thomas P. Novak, Donna L. Hoffman, and Yiu-Fai Yung, "Measuring the Customer Experience in Online Environments: A Structural Modeling Approach," *Marketing Science* 19, no. 1 (2000): 22.

14. Bill Hensel, "Airline Alliance Expands: Continental Part of International Sky Team Group," *Houston Chronicle*, September 14, 2004, 1.

15. Naomi Aoki, "Beyond the Bag," *Boston Globe*, September 26, 2004, B1.

16. James P. Carse, *Finite and Infinite Games* (New York: Ballantine Books, 1994).

17. Shona L. Brown and Kathleen M. Eisenhardt, *Competing on the Edge: Strategy as Structured Chaos* (Cambridge, Mass.: Harvard Business School Press, 1998), 10.

18. Tom Stemberg and David Whiteford, "Putting a Stop to Mom and Pop," *FSB: Fortune Small Business* 12, no. 8 (2002): 38.

19. Bluedorn, *Human Organization of Time*, 50.

20. Carol Kaufman-Scarborough and Jay D. Lindquist, "Time Management and Polychronicity: Comparisons, Contrasts, and In-

sights for the Workplace," *Journal of Managerial Psychology* 14, no. 3/4 (1999): 288–312.

21. Robert D. Putnam, *Bowling Alone: The Collapse and Revival of American Community* (New York: Simon & Schuster, 2000), 331.

22. David Harris, "Pete Rozelle: The Man Who Made Football an American Obsession," *New York Times Magazine*, January 15, 1984, 14.

23. Dick Daniels, "Leadership Lessons from Championship Basketball," *Journal for Quality and Participation* 19, no. 3 (1996): 36.

24. Robert W. Keidel, *Game Plans: Sports Strategies for Business* (New York: E. P. Dutton, 1985), 57.

25. Stanley M. Davis, *Future Perfect* (Reading, Mass.: Addison-Wesley, 1990), 26.

CHAPTER 3

1. Arkalgud Ramaprasad and Wayne G. Stone, "The Temporal Dimension of Strategy," *Time & Society* 1, no. 3 (1992): 359.

2. For a fascinating investigation of this idea, see Gregory F. Hayden, "The Evolution of Time Constructs and Their Impact on Socio-Economic Planning," *Journal of Economic Issues* 21, no. 3 (1987): 1281–1312.

3. Linda Greenlaw, *The Hungry Ocean: A Swordboat Captain's Journal* (New York: Hyperion, 2000), 45.

4. Mark Davis and Janelle Heineke, "Understanding the Roles of the Customer and the Operation for Better Queue Management," *International Journal of Operations and Production Management* 14, no. 5 (1994): 21–35.

5. For a discussion of the benefits of combined queues, see D. R. Smith and W. Whitt, "On the Efficiency of Shared Resources in Queuing Systems," *Bell Systems Technology Journal* 60 (January 1981): 39–57. For examples of situations where feeder lines are not desirable, see M. H. Rothkopf and P. Rech, "Perspectives on Queues: Combining Queues Is Not Always Beneficial," *Operations Research* 35, no. 6 (1987): 906–909. Grocery stores,

for example, tend not to use combined queues largely because of the physical issues involved with relatively large, difficult-to-maneuver grocery carts.

6. M. M. Davis and T. E. Vollmann, "A Framework for Relating Waiting Time and Customer Satisfaction in a Service Operation," *Journal of Services Marketing* 4, no. 1 (Winter 1990): 61–69.

7. Of course, if the wait actually takes an hour, Julie will be upset no matter what; people will accept a slightly unreliable estimate, but they rightly expect competence and honesty here, as in every aspect of the restaurant's operation.

8. As cited in Edward T. Hall, *The Dance of Life: The Other Dimension of Time* (Garden City, N.Y.: Anchor Press/Doubleday, 1983).

9. William Powell, "Like Life? Simulations Are Poised to Change the Direction of E-Learning. But Who Will Take the Wheel?" *T + D* (February 2002): 34–36.

10. Keith H. Hammonds, "Pay as You Go: Mobil Launched Speedpass to Help Customers Guzzle Gas Faster," *Fast Company*, no. 52 (2001): 46.

11. George Stalk, Jr., and Thomas M. Hout, *Competing Against Time: How Time-Based Competition Is Reshaping Global Markets* (New York: Free Press, 1990), 4.

12. Megan Williams, "Ode to Slow: The Italian 'Slow Movement' Is Spreading Around the Globe as Towns and Small Cities Put Up Cultural Barricades to Fight the Tide of Globalization," (Toronto) *Globe and Mail*, April 28, 2001, 1.

13. Annick Moes and Neal E. Boudette, "Pipe Dreams: Here's a Concert Even Diehards Can't Sit Through: Played Slowly, John Cage Opus Will Last for 639 Years: Intermission in 2319," *Wall Street Journal*, July 11, 2003, A1.

14. Ibid.

15. Meyer Friedman and Ray H. Resenmar, *Type A Behavior and Your Heart* (New York: Knopf, 1974), 60.

16. Larry A. Pace and Waino W. Suojanen, "Addictive Type A Behavior Undermines Employee Involvement," *Personnel Journal* 67, no. 6 (1988): 40. See also Amanda Bennett, "Type A

Managers Stuck in the Middle," *Wall Street Journal,* June 17, 1988, 17.

17. Christine Y. Chen, "The Last-Mover Advantage," *Fortune* 144, no. 1 (2001): 84.

18. E. B. Fein, "Earthquake Toll Staggers Soviets," *St. Petersburg Times,* August 29, 1994, 8A. Quoted in Michael Flaherty, *A Watched Pot: How We Experience Time* (New York: New York University Press, 1999), 51.

19. Michael Murphy and John Brody, "I Experience a Kind of Clarity," *Intellectual Digest* 3 (1973): 19–20. Quoted in Michael Flaherty, *A Watched Pot: How We Experience Time* (New York: New York University Press, 1999), 75.

20. Charles Darwin, *The Life and Letters of Charles Darwin,* Vol. 1, ed. F. Darwin (1888; reprint, New York: Basic Books, 1959), 29. Quoted in Michael Flaherty, *A Watched Pot: How We Experience Time* (New York: New York University Press, 1999), 75.

21. In all, Flaherty identified six causes: Suffering and Intense Emotions; Violence and Danger; Waiting and Boredom; Altered States; Concentration and Meditation; and Shock and Novelty.

22. Bill Breen, "I Can Only Compete Through My Crew," *Fast Company,* no. 40 (2000): 270.

23. "The Price of Lateness: Ecuadorean Time," *Economist* 369, no. 8351 (2003): 67.

24. Katie Zernike, "Cell Phones Absolving Hang-ups About Tardiness, Study Says," *Houston Chronicle,* November 6, 2003, 5.

CHAPTER 4

1. Art in Rhythm, www.artinrhythm.com. Accessed May 15, 2003.

2. Edward T. Hall, *The Dance of Life: The Other Dimension of Time* (Garden City, N.Y.: Anchor Press/Doubleday, 1983), 152–153.

3. Ibid., 156.

4. Jeremy Campbell, *Winston Churchill's Afternoon Nap* (New York: Simon & Schuster, 1986), 235.

5. Nicholas Wade, "We Got Rhythm: The Mystery Is How and Why," *New York Times,* September 16, 2003, F1.

6. João Vieira Da Cunha, Mary Crossan, et al., "Time and Organizational Improvisation," paper presented at the Dynamic Time and Creative Inquiry in Organizational Change Conference, Boston, Mass., June 18–21, 2002.

7. Quoted in Josie Glausiusz, "Joining Hands—The Mathematics of Applause," *Discover* 21, no. 7 (2000): 32–33.

8. Deborah Ancona and Chee-Leong Chong, "Entrainment: Pace, Cycle, and Rhythm in Organizational Behavior," *Research in Organizational Behavior* 18 (1996): 251–284.

9. James Sorowiecki, "The Most Devastating Retailer in the World," *New Yorker* 76, no. 27 (2000): 74.

10. Phil Jackson and H. Delehanty, *Sacred Hoops: Spiritual Lessons of a Hardwood Warrior* (New York: Hyperion, 1995), 98–99.

11. Naomi Aoki, "Beyond the Bag," *Boston Globe*, September 26, 2004, B1.

12. Allen C. Bluedorn, "The Clock of Charles V and the Organization of the World," paper presented at the Future of Time in Management and Organizations conference, Fontainebleau, France, July 7, 2004. See also Allen C. Bluedorn, *The Human Organization of Time: Temporal Realities and Experience* (Stanford, Calif.: Stanford University Press, 2002), 157–160.

13. Daniel Roth, "The Trophy Life," *Fortune* 149, no. 8 (2004): 70.

14. Shona L. Brown and Kathleen M. Eisenhardt, *Competing on the Edge: Strategy as Structured Chaos* (Cambridge, Mass.: Harvard Business School Press, 1998), 15–17.

15. Lauretta McLeod and Steven Freeman, "Organizational Leadership Lessons from Argentine Tango," paper presented at the Second Improvisational Conference on the Future of Time in Management and Organizations, Fontainebleau, France, July 7, 2004.

16. William Felton and Bill Russell, *Second Wind: The Memoirs of an Opinionated Man* (New York: Random House, 1979).

CHAPTER 5

1. Quoted in Samuel L. Macey, "Clock Metaphor," in *The Encyclopedia of Time*, ed. Samuel L. Macey (New York and London: Garland Publishing, 1994), 118.

2. John Postill, "Clock and Calendar Time: A Missing Anthropo-logical Problem," *Time & Society* 11, no. 2/3 (2002): 250.

3. John E. Smith, "Time and Qualitative Time," in *Rhetoric and Kairos: Essays in History, Theory and Praxis*, ed. Phillip Sipiora and James S. Baumlin, (Albany: State University of New York Press, 2002), 47.

4. Charles Dickens, *Hard Times* (1854; reprint, New York: Oxford University Press, 1989), 1.

5. Andy Dumaine, "Where's the Intuition?" *Adweek* 44, no. 19 (2003): 25.

6. This anecdote is related by John Kay, "Beware the Pitfalls of Over-Reliance on Rationality," *Financial Times*, August 20, 2002, 9.

7. See, for instance, Brian Bloch, "In Your Guts Doesn't Mean It's Nuts," *Guardian* (London), March 13, 2004, Jobs and Money Pages, 28; and Stephen Overell, "Why Sixth Sense Is the Next Big Thing for Business," *Financial Times*, October 6, 2001, Off Centre, 10.

8. Greg A. Stevens and James Burley, "Piloting the Rocket of Radical Innovation," *Research Technology Management* 46, no. 2 (2003): 16–25.

9. "The Type Preferences," www.MyersBriggs.org, accessed June 21, 2004.

10. Gary Klein, *Sources of Power: How People Make Decisions* (Boston: MIT Press, 1997). Klein follows up on this topic with *Intuition at Work* (New York: Currency Doubleday, 2003).

11. Andrew S. Grove, *Only the Paranoid Survive* (New York: Currency, 1996), 33.

12. Ibid., 89.

13. Ibid., 35.

14. We are reminded again of the research we mentioned in Chapter 3 regarding the predominance in middle management of type A personalities (defined primarily as having a "sense of time urgency") and the predominance in upper management of type Bs.

CHAPTER 6

1. Dilap Soman, "The Mental Accounting of Sunk Time Costs: Why Time Is Not Like Money," *Journal of Behavioral Decision Making* 14, no. 3 (2001): 14.

2. Henri Bergson, *Time and Free Will: An Essay on the Immediate Data of Consciousness* (London: G. Allen and Company, 1959).

3. Robert B. Tucker, "Ilya Prigogine: Wizard of Time," introduction to May 1983 interview on http://www.edu365.com/aula-net/comsoc/visions/documentos/interview_prigogine1983.htm, accessed May 4, 2004.

4. George Hudson, "Concerted Flashing of Fireflies," *Science* 48 (1918): 573–575.

5. Ibid.

6. One of our favorite illustrations of capitalist spontaneous order is contained in the ABC News Special "Greed: Is It Necessarily Bad?" in which correspondent John Stossel follows a beefsteak from hoof to plate, explaining how it gets there. "Greed" is available on videotape from Films for the Humanities & Sciences.

7. Margaret Wheatley, *Leadership and the New Science: Learning About Organizations from an Orderly Universe* (San Francisco: Berrett-Koehler, 1992), 77–78.

8. Associated Press, "Tampa Shows Less Can Be More," (Oneonta, N.Y.) *Daily Star*, June 9, 2004.

9. Academy of Achievement, Interview with Oprah Winfrey, available at www.achievement.org/autodoc/page/win0int-4, accessed August 18, 2004. Copyright 2004.

10. Arthur Schnabel, quoted in Sydney J. Harris, "It's the Pause That Counts in Art," *Chicago Daily News*, June 11, 1958, p. 18.

BIBLIOGRAPHY

Adam, Barbara. *Time and Social Theory*. Philadelphia: Temple University Press, 1990.

———. *Time*. Cambridge, UK: Polity Press, 2004.

Adams, Gary A., and Steve M. Jex. "Relationships Between Time Management, Control, Work-Family Conflict, and Strain." *Journal of Occupational Health Psychology* 4, no. 1 (1999): 72–77.

Amabile, Teresa M., Constance N. Hadley, and Steven J. Kramer. "Creativity Under the Gun." *Harvard Business Review* 80, no. 8 (2002): 52.

Ancona, Deborah, and Chee-Leong Chong, "Entrainment: Pace, Cycle, and Rhythm in Organizational Behavior." *Research in Organizational Behavior* 18 (1996): 251–284.

Angell, Roger, and Elizabeth V. Warren. *The Perfect Game: America Looks at Baseball*. New York: Harry N. Abrams, 2003.

Aoki, Naomi. "Beyond the Bag." *Boston Globe*, September 26, 2004, B1.

Associated Press. "Tampa Shows Less Can Be More." (Oneonta, N.Y.) *Daily Star*, June 9, 2004.

Aveni, Anthony F. *Empires of Time: Calendars, Clocks, and Cultures*. New York: Basic Books, 1989.

Barling, Julian, Dominic Cheung, and E. Kevin Kelloway. "Time Management and Achievement Striving Interact to Predict Car Sales Performance." *Journal of Applied Psychology* 81, no. 6 (1996): 821–826.

Barnett, Jo Ellen. *Time's Pendulum: The Quest to Capture Time—From Sundials to Atomic Clocks.* New York: Plenum Press, 1998.

Bartunek, Jean M., and Raul A. Necochea. "Old Insights and New Times: Kairos, Inca Cosmology and Their Contributions to Contemporary Management Inquiry." *Journal of Management Inquiry* 9, no. 2 (2000): 103–112.

Bender, John, and David E. Wellbery (eds.). *Chronotypes: The Construction of Time.* Stanford, Calif.: Stanford University Press, 1991.

Bennett, Amanda. "Type A Managers Stuck in the Middle." *Wall Street Journal,* June 17, 1988, 17.

Bennis, Warren, and Burt Nanus. *Leaders: The Strategies for Taking Charge.* New York: HarperBusiness, 1997.

Berger, John. *Ways of Seeing.* Reprint, New York: Viking Press, 1995.

Bergson, Henri. *Time and Free Will: An Essay on the Immediate Data of Consciousness.* London: George Allen & Unwin Ltd., 1959.

Berlin, Sir Isaiah. *The Hedgehog and the Fox.* New York: Simon & Schuster, 1953.

Blaise, Clark. *Time Lord: Sir Sandford Fleming and the Creation of Standard Time.* New York: Pantheon Books, 2000.

Bloch, Brian. "In Your Guts Doesn't Mean It's Nuts." *Guardian* (London), March 13, 2004, Jobs and Money Pages, 28.

Bluedorn, Allen C. *The Human Organization of Time: Temporal Realities and Experience.* Stanford, Calif.: Stanford Business Books, 2002.

———. "The Clock of Charles V and the Organization of the World." Paper presented at the Future of Time in Management and Organizations conference, Fontainebleau, France, July 7, 2004.

Boorstin, Daniel J. *The Discoverers*. New York: Random House, 1983.

Bradenburger, Adam M., and Barry J. Nalebuff. *Co-Opetition: A Revolution Mindset That Combines Competition and Cooperation: The Game Theory Strategy That's Changing the Game of Business*. New York: Currency/Doubleday, 1997.

Brand, Stewart. "Taking the Long View." *Time* 155, no. 17 (2000): 86.

———. "The Long Now Foundation: Goals," www.longnow.org/about/about.htm. Accessed February 13, 2004.

Breen, Bill, "I Can Only Compete Through My Crew." *Fast Company*, no. 40 (2000).

Bronowski, Jacob. *The Ascent of Man*. Boston: Little, Brown, 1974.

Bronson, Po. "The Long Now." *Wired* 6, no. 5 (1998): 116–139.

Brown, Shona L., and Kathleen M. Eisenhardt. *Competing on the Edge: Strategy as Structured Chaos*. Cambridge, Mass.: Harvard Business School Press, 1998.

Campbell, Don. *The Mozart Effect: Tapping the Power of Music to Heal the Body, Strengthen the Mind, and Unlock the Creative Spirit*. New York: Avon Books, 1997.

Campbell, Jeremy. *Winston Churchill's Afternoon Nap*. New York: Simon & Schuster, 1986.

Carse, James P. *Finite and Infinite Games*. New York: The Free Press, 1986.

Church, Margaret. *Time and Reality: Studies in Contemporary Fiction*. Chapel Hill: University of North Carolina Press, 1963.

Clark, Peter. "A Review of the Theories of Time and Structure for Organizational Sociology." *Research in the Sociology of Organizations* 4 (1985): 35–79.

Clayman, Steven E. "The Production of Punctuality: Social Interaction, Temporal Organization, and Social Structure." *American Journal of Sociology* 95, no. 3 (1989): 671.

Collins, Jim. "Leadership Lessons of a Rock Climber." *Fast Company*, no. 77 (2003): 109–110.

Csikszentmihalyi, Mihaly. *Beyond Boredom and Anxiety: Experiencing Flow in Work and Play*. San Francisco: Jossey-Bass, 1975.

———. *Flow: The Psychology of Optimal Experience.* New York: Harper Perennial, 1991.

———. *Good Business: Leadership, Flow, and the Making of Meaning.* New York: Viking Penguin, 2003.

Csikszentmihalyi, Mihaly, and Isabella Selega Csikszentmihalyi (eds.). *Optimal Experience: Psychological Studies of Flow in Consciousness.* Cambridge, U.K.: Cambridge University Press, 1998.

Da Cunha, João Vieira, Mary Crossan, et al. "Time and Organizational Improvisation." Paper presented at the Dynamic Time and Creative Inquiry in Organizational Change Conference, Boston, Mass., June 18–21, 2002.

Daniels, Dick. "Leadership Lessons from Championship Basketball." *Journal for Quality and Participation* 19, no. 3 (1996): 36.

Darwin, Charles. *On the Origin of Species by Means of Natural Selection: or, The Preservation of Favoured Races in the Struggle for Life.* London: J. Murray, 1859.

———. *The Life and Letters of Charles Darwin,* Vol. 1. Edited by F. Darwin. 1888. Reprint, New York: Basic Books, 1959. Quoted in Michael Flaherty, *A Watched Pot: How We Experience Time.* New York: New York University Press, 1999, 75.

Davies, Paul. *About Time: Einstein's Unfinished Revolution.* New York: Simon & Schuster, 1995.

Davis, M. M., and T. E. Vollmann. "A Framework for Relating Waiting Time and Customer Satisfaction in a Service Operation." *Journal of Services Marketing* 4, no. 1 (Winter 1990): 61–69.

Davis, Mark, and Janelle Heineke. "Understanding the Roles of the Customer and the Operation for Better Queue Management." *International Journal of Operations and Production Management* 14, no. 5 (1994): 21–35.

Davis, Stanley M. *Future Perfect.* Reading, Mass.: Addison-Wesley, 1987.

De Botton, Alain. *How Proust Can Change Your Life.* New York: Vintage Books, 1998.

De Graaf, John (ed.). *Take Back Your Time: Fighting Overwork and Time Poverty in America.* San Francisco: Berrett-Koehler, 2003.

Deutsch, Diana (ed.). *The Psychology of Music*. New York: Academic Press, 1982.

Dickens, Charles. *Hard Times*. 1854. Reprint, New York: Oxford University Press, 1989.

Drucker, Peter. *Managing in a Time of Great Change*. New York: Truman Talley Books/Dutton, 1995.

Dumaine, Andy. "Where's the Intuition?" *Adweek* 44, no. 19 (2003): 25.

Einstein, Albert. *Relativity*. New York: Crown, 1961.

Eriksen, Thomas Hylland. *Tyranny of the Moment: Fast and Slow Time in the Information Age*. London: Pluto Press, 2001.

Faulkner, William. *The Sound and the Fury*. New York: Vintage Press, 1991.

Fein, E. B. "Earthquake Toll Staggers Soviets." *St. Petersburg Times*, August 29, 1994, 8A. Quoted in Michael Flaherty, *A Watched Pot: How We Experience Time*. New York: New York University Press, 1999, 51.

Felton, Willam, and Bill Russell. *Second Wind: The Memoirs of an Opinionated Man*. New York: Random House, 1979.

Flaherty, Michael. *A Watched Pot: How We Experience Time*. New York: New York University Press, 1999.

Flood, Raymond, and Michael Lockwood (eds.). *The Nature of Time*. Oxford: Basil Blackwell Ltd., 1986.

Fraser, J. T. (ed.). *The Voices of Time: A Cooperative Survey of Man's Views of Time as Expressed by the Sciences and by the Humanities*. New York: George Braziller, 1966.

———. *The Genesis and Evolution of Time*. Amherst: University of Massachusetts Press, 1982.

———. *Time the Familiar Stranger*. Amherst: University of Massachusetts Press, 1987.

———. "Human Temporality in a Nowless Universe." *Time & Society* 1, no. 2 (1992): 159–173.

———. *Time, Conflict, and Human Values*. Urbana and Chicago: University of Illinois Press, 1999.

Friedman, Meyer, and Ray H. Resenmar. *Type A Behavior and Your Heart*. New York: Knopf, 1974.

Friedman, William J. *About Time: Inventing the Fourth Dimension.* Cambridge, Mass.: MIT Press, 1990.

Gardner, Howard, Mihaly Csikszentmihalyi, and William Damon. *Good Work: When Excellence and Ethics Meet.* New York: Basic Books, 2001.

Gleick, James. *Chaos: Making a New Science.* New York: Viking, 1987.

———. *Faster: The Acceleration of Just About Everything.* New York: Vintage Books, 2000.

Gold, Matea. "The Race to the White House: Dean Campaigns in the Past Tense." *Los Angeles Times,* February 17, 2004, A15.

Gott, J. Richard. *Time Travel in Einstein's Universe: The Physical Possibilities of Travel Through Time.* New York: Houghton Mifflin, 2001.

Graig, William Lane. "God and Real Time." *Religious Studies* 26 (1990): 335–347.

Greenlaw, Linda. *The Hungry Ocean: A Swordboat Captain's Journal.* New York: Hyperion, 2000.

Grove, Andrew S. *Only the Paranoid Survive.* New York: Currency, 1996.

Hajdu, David. "Wynton's Blues." *Atlantic Monthly* 291, no. 2 (2003): 43–55.

Hall, Edward T. *The Silent Language.* Garden City, N.Y.: Doubleday, 1959.

———. *Beyond Culture.* Garden City, N.Y.: Anchor Press/Doubleday, 1977.

———. *The Dance of Life: The Other Dimension of Time.* Garden City, N.Y.: Anchor Press/Doubleday, 1983.

Hall, Edward T., and Mildred Reed Hall. *Understanding Cultural Differences.* Yarmouth, Me.: Intercultural Press, 1990.

Hammonds, Keith H. "Michael Porter's Big Ideas." *Fast Company,* no. 44 (2001): 150.

———. "Pay as You Go: Mobil Launched Speedpass to Help Customers Guzzle Gas Faster." *Fast Company,* no. 52 (2001): 44–46.

actional Sky Team Group." *Houston Chronicle*, September 14, 2004, 1.

Holden, Constance. "Your Words Betray You." *Science* 300, no. 5619 (April 25, 2003): 577.

Holson, Laura M. "Bold Rising Star at Lockheed Is Point Man on Prize Contract." *New York Times,* November 1, 2001, C1.

Hunt, Albert R. "The U.N. to Bush's Rescue?" *Wall Street Journal,* April 22, 2004, A19.

Inwood, Michael. "Aristotle on the Reality of Time." In *Aristotle's Physics,* edited by Lindsay Judson. Oxford: Clarendon Press, 1991.

Jackson, Phil, and H. Delehanty. *Sacred Hoops: Spiritual Lessons of a Hardwood Warrior.* New York: Hyperion, 1995.

Jackson, Susan A., and Mihaly Csikszentmihalyi. *Flow in Sports: The Keys to Optimal Experiences and Performances.* Champaign, Ill.: Human Kinetics, 1999.

Jantsch, Erich. *Self-Organizing Universe: Scientific and Human Implications.* Oxford: Pergamon Press, 1980.

Johnson, George. *A Shortcut Through Time: The Path to the Quantum Computer.* New York: Alfred A. Knopf, 2003.

Johnson, Spencer. *The Present: The Gift That Makes You Happy and Successful at Work and in Life.* New York: Doubleday, 2003.

Jordan, Robert. "Time and Contingency in St. Augustine." In *Augustine: A Collection of Critical Essays,* edited by R. A. Markus. Garden City, N.Y.: Anchor Press, 1972.

Kanter, Rosabeth Moss. *The Change Masters*. New York: Simon & Schuster, 1983.

Kaufman-Scarborough, Carol, and Jay D. Lindquist. "Time Management and Polychronicity: Comparisons, Contrasts, and Insights for the Workplace." *Journal of Managerial Psychology* 14, no. 3/4 (1999): 288–312.

Kay, John. "Beware the Pitfalls of Over-Reliance on Rationality." *Financial Times,* August 20, 2002, 9.

Keidel, Robert W. *Game Plans: Sports Strategies for Business*. New York: E. P. Dutton, 1985.

Keyssar, Alexander, and Ernest May. "Education for Public Service in the United States: A History." In *For the People: Can We Fix Public Service?* edited by John D. Donahue and Joseph S. Nye, Jr. Washington, D.C.: Brookings Institution, 2003.

Klein, Gary. *Sources of Power: How People Make Decisions*. Boston: MIT Press, 1997.

———. *Intuition at Work*. New York: Currency Doubleday, 2003.

Kornheiser, Tony. "Question with Authority." *Washington Post,* February 26, 2004, D1.

Kotter, John P. (ed.). "What Effective General Managers Really Do." *Harvard Business Review* 77, no. 2, 145–156.

Kramer, Jonathan D. *The Time of Music: New Meanings, New Temporalities, New Listening Strategies*. New York: Schirmer Books, 1988.

Krier, Beth Ann. *Los Angeles Times* [Home Edition], December 14, 1986.

Landes, David S. *Revolution in Time*. Cambridge, Mass.: Belknap Press of Harvard University Press, 2000.

Lapierre, Dominique, and Larry Collins. *Freedom at Midnight*. New Delhi: Vikas Publishing House, 2001.

Lauer, Robert H. *Temporal Man: The Meaning and Uses of Social Time*. New York: Praeger, 1981.

Levine, Robert V. "The Pace of Life." *American Scientist* 78 (1990): 450–459.

———. *A Geography of Time: The Temporal Misadventures of a Social Psychologist, or How Every Culture Keeps Time Just a Little Bit Differently*. New York: Basic Books, 1997.

Lippincott, Kristen. *The Story of Time*. London: Merrell Holberton Publishers Ltd., 1999.

Lowe, Janet. *Jack Welch Speaks: Wisdom from the World's Greatest Business Leader*. New York: John Wiley & Sons, 2001.

Lundin, Robert W. *An Objective Psychology of Music*. New York: Ronald Press Company, 1967.

Macan, Therese Hoff. "Time Management: Test of a Process Model." *Journal of Applied Psychology* 79, no. 3 (1994): 381–391.

Macan, Therese H., Comila Shahani, Robert L. Dipboye, and Amanda P. Phillips. "College Students' Time Management: Correlations with Academic Performance and Stress." *Journal of Educational Psychology* 82, no. 4 (1990): 760–768.

Macey, Samuel L. *Clocks and the Cosmos: Time in Western Life and Thought*. Hamden, Conn.: Archon Books, 1980.

Macey, Samuel L. (ed.). *The Encyclopedia of Time*. New York and London: Garland Publishing, 1994.

Mainzer, Klaus. *The Little Book of Time*. New York: Springer-Verlag, 2002.

March, James G. "Exploration and Exploitation in Organizational Learning." *Organization Science* 2 (1991): 71–87.

Martin, Russell. *Picasso's War: The Destruction of Guernica, and the Masterpiece That Changed the World*. New York: Dutton, 2002.

McGrath, Joseph Edward (ed.). *The Social Psychology of Time: New Perspectives*. Newbury Park, Calif.: Sage, 1988.

McLeod, Lauretta, and Steven Freeman. "Organizational Leadership Lessons from Argentine Tango." Paper presented at the Second Improvisational Conference on the Future of Time in Management and Organizations, Fontainebleau, France, July 7–12, 2004.

McLuhan, Marshall, and Phillip B. Meggs. *The Mechanical Bride: Folklore of Industrial Man*. Corte Madera, Calif.: Gingko Press, 2002.

Mead, George Herbert. *The Philosophy of the Present*. Edited by Arthur E. Murphy. La Salle, Ill.: Open Court Publishing Company, 1959.

Meerloo, Joost A. M. *Along the Fourth Dimension*. New York: John Day Company, 1970.

Meyerhoff, Hans. *Time in Literature*. Berkeley: University of California Press, 1955.

Miller, Donald F. "Political Time: The Problem of Timing and Chance." *Time & Society* 2, no. 2 (1993): 179–197.

Moes, Annick, and Neal E. Boudette. "Pipe Dreams: Here's a Concert Even Diehards Can't Sit Through: Played Slowly, John Cage Opus Will Last for 639 Years: Intermission in 2319." *Wall Street Journal*, July 11, 2003, A1.

Moore, Shirley. *Biological Clocks and Patterns*. New York: Criterion Books, 1967.

Murphy, Michael, and John Brody. "I Experience a Kind of Clarity." *Intellectual Digest* 3 (1973), 19–20. Quoted in Michael Flaherty, *A Watched Pot: How We Experience Time*. New York: New York University Press, 1999, 75.

Neustadt, Richard E. *Thinking in Time: The Uses of History for Decision Makers*. New York: Free Press, 1988.

Newton, Roger G. *Galileo's Pendulum: From the Rhythm of Time to the Making of Matter*. Cambridge, Mass.: Harvard University Press, 2004.

Novak, Thomas P., Donna L. Hoffman, and Yiu-Fai Yung. "Measuring the Customer Experience in Online Environments: A Structural Modeling Approach." *Marketing Science* 19, no. 1 (2000): 22.

O'Brian, Patrick. *Post Captain*. New York: Norton, 1972.

Ornstein, Robert E. *On the Experience of Time*. Hammondsworth, U.K.: Penguin, 1969.

Overell, Stephen. "Why Sixth Sense Is the Next Big Thing for Business." *Financial Times* (London), October 6, 2001, Off Centre, 10.

Pace, Larry A., and Waino W. Suojanen. "Addictive Type A Behavior Undermines Employee Involvement." *Personnel Journal* 67, no. 6 (1988): 36–40.

Parker, Ian. "Absolute PowerPoint: The Annals of Business." *New Yorker* 77, no. 13 (2001): 76–87.

Patrides, C. A. *Aspects of Time*. Manchester, U.K.: Manchester University Press, 1976.

Poulet, Georges. *Studies in Human Time*. Translated by Elliott Coleman. Baltimore: John Hopkins Press, 1956.

Prigogine, Ilya, and Isabelle Stengers. *Order out of Chaos: Man's New Dialogue with Nature*. Boulder, Colo.: New Science Library, 1984.

Purser, Ronald E., and Jack Petranker. "Unfreezing the Future: Utilizing Dynamic Time for Deep Improvisation in Organizational Change." Paper presented at the Dynamic Time and Creative Inquiry in Organizational Change Conference, Boston, Mass., June 18–21, 2002.

Putnam, Robert D. *Bowling Alone: The Collapse and Revival of American Community*. New York: Simon & Schuster, 2000.

Ramaprasad, Arkalgud, and Wayne G. Stone. "The Temporal Dimension of Strategy." *Time & Society* 1, no. 3 (1992): 359.

Rechtschaffen, Stephen. *Timeshifting: Creating More Time to Enjoy Your Life*. New York: Broadway Books, 2002.

Riesman, David, with Nathan Glazer and Reuel Denny. *The Lonely Crowd*. New Haven and London: Yale University Press, 1961.

Robinson, James W. *Jack Welch on Leadership: Executive Lessons from the Master CEO*. New York: Precidio, 2001.

Roth, Daniel. "The Trophy Life." *Fortune* 149, no. 8 (2004): 70.

Rothkopf, M. H., and P. Rech. "Perspectives on Queues: Combining Queues Is Not Always Beneficial." *Operations Research* 35, no. 6 (1987): 906–909.

Sabelis, Ida. "Time Management: Paradoxes and Patterns." *Time & Society* 10, no. 2/3 (2001): 387–400.

Sandberg, Jared. "To-Do Lists Can Take More Time Than Doing, but That Isn't the Point." *Wall Street Journal*, September 8, 2004, B1.

Schall, Jan (ed.). *Tempus Fugit: Time Flies*. Catalogue published in conjunction with the exhibit of the same name at the Nelson-Atkins Museum of Art, Kansas City, Missouri, 2000.

Schneider, Manuel. "Time at High Altitude: Experiencing Time on the Roof of the World." *Time & Society* 11, no. 1 (2002): 140–146.

Shallis, Michael. *On Time: An Investigation Into Scientific Knowledge and Human Experience.* New York: Schocken Books, 1983.

Slater, Robert. *Jack Welch and the GE Way: Management Insights and Leadership Secrets of the Legendary CEO.* New York: McGraw-Hill, 1999.

Smith, D. R., and W. Whitt. "On the Efficiency of Shared Resources in Queuing Systems." *Bell Systems Technology Journal* 60 (January 1981): 39–57.

Smith, John E. "Time and Qualitative Time." In *Rhetoric and Kairos: Essays in History, Theory, and Praxis,* edited by Phillip Sipiora and James S. Baumlin. Albany: State University of New York Press, 2002.

Smith, Quentin. *Language and Time.* New York: Oxford University Press, 1993.

Soman, Dilap. "The Mental Accounting of Sunk Time Costs: Why Time Is Not Like Money." *Journal of Behavioral Decision Making* 14, no. 3 (2001): 14.

Sorowiecki, James. "The Most Devastating Retailer in the World." *New Yorker* 76, no. 27 (2000): 74.

Stalk, George, Jr. and Thomas M. Hout. *Competing Against Time: How Time-Based Competition Is Reshaping Global Markets.* New York: Free Press, 1990.

Stenger, Victor J. *Timeless Reality: Symmetry, Simplicity, and Multiple Universes.* Amherst, N.Y.: Prometheus Books, 2000.

Stevens, Greg A., and James Burley. "Piloting the Rocket of Radical Innovation." *Research Technology Management* 46, no. 2 (2003): 16–25.

Strogatz, Steven. *Sync: The Emerging Science of Spontaneous Order.* New York: Hyperion, 2003.

Talon, Henri. "Space, Time, and Memory in *Great Expectations.*" *Dickens Studies Annual* 3 (1973): 122–133.

Tam, Pui-Wing. "Rebooting in a Tough Market, a Tech Executive Chooses to Gamble." *Wall Street Journal,* January 24, 2003, A1.

Thaler, R. H. "Toward a Positive Theory of Consumer Choice." *Journal of Economic Behavior and Organization* 1 (1980): 39–60.

———. "Mental Accounting and Consumer Choice." *Marketing Science* 4 (1985): 199–214.

———. "Mental Accounting Matters." *Journal of Behavioral Decision Making* 12 (1999): 183–206.

Useem, Jerry. "Another Boss Another Revolution." *Fortune* 149, no. 7 (2004): 112–124.

Wade, Nicholas. "We Got Rhythm: The Mystery Is How and Why." *New York Times*, September 16, 2003, F1.

Waterhouse, James. "Light Dawns on the Body Clock." *New Scientist* 132, no. 1792 (1991): 30–34.

Weinberg, Steven. *The First Three Minutes: A Modern View of the Origin of the Universe.* New York: Basic Books, 1977.

Wheatley, Margaret J. *Leadership and the New Science: Learning About Organization from an Orderly Universe.* San Francisco: Berrett-Koehler, 1992.

White, Eric Charles. *Kaironomia: On the Will-to-Invent.* Ithaca, N.Y.: Cornell University Press, 1987.

Wilcox, Donald J. *The Measure of Times Past: Pre-Newtonian Chronologies and the Rhetoric of Relative Time.* Chicago: University of Chicago Press, 1987.

Williams, Megan. "Ode to Slow: The Italian 'Slow Movement' Is Spreading Around the Globe as Towns and Small Cities Put Up Cultural Barricades to Fight the Tide of Globalization." (Toronto) *Globe and Mail*, April 28, 2001.

Wood, Douglas Kellogg. *Men Against Time.* Lawrence: University Press of Kansas, 1982.

Wright, Karen. "Times of Our Lives." *Scientific American* Special Issue (September 2002): 58–65.

Wright, Lawrence. *Clockwork Man: The Story of Time: Its Origins, Its Uses, Its Tyranny.* New York: Horizon Press, 1969.

Young, Michael. *The Metronomic Society.* Cambridge, Mass.: Harvard University Press, 1988.

INDEX

routine complexity, 66–69
runners, 101
Russell, Bill, 118

sailing, 41–42, 62–66,
    121–122
St. Louis, Martin, 163
Sapporo, 48
Saturnini, Paolo, 79–80
Saving Private Ryan (film),
    86–87
scaling down, 73–75
Schnabel, Arthur, 165, 166
Science (journal), 157–158,
    159
scientific management, 28,
    161
Second Wind (Russell), 118
self-organizing systems,
    157–161, 169
shared rhythm, *see* entrain-
    ment
shareholder value maximi-
    zation, 18, 28
Siegel, Art, 39
silent films, 137
simulations, 73–79
    critics of, 76
    management develop-
        ment programs, 75–77
    scaling down in, 73–75
singing, endorphins from,
    97

slowing down, 79–82, 84–
    85, 91, 103–104
slow-motion effect, 84–87
    examples of, 84–85
    in leadership, 85–87
Smith, Adam, 9, 159
Smith, John E., 124
Smith, Malcolm, 95
social bonding, 97
social networks, 52
Soman, Dilap, 151–154
Sophocles, 88
Sound and the Fury, The
    (Faulkner), 90
Sources of Power (Klein),
    133
Southwest Airlines, 44
Soviet Union, former, five-
    year economic plans,
    160
Spain, tempo entrainment at
    Zara, 102–103
special theory of relativity
    (Einstein), 63
Speedpass, 78
Spielberg, Steven, 86–87
spontaneity, 50–51
sports, continuous flow in,
    53–56
spreadsheets, 129–130
Squibb, 47
Stalk, George, Jr., 78–79
Staples, 49–50
Stemberg, Tom, 49–50

Not just lectures,
but the human touch.

Not just theory,
but tools you can use.

That's the
AMA difference.
Come learn with us.

109239

FREE! Get the American Management
Association's Latest Catalog.

Fill out and return this postage-paid card

OR... fax it to 1-518-891-0368.

OR... call 1-800-262-9699 and mention priority code XBDQ.

OR... go to www.amanet.org

Name _____

Title _____

Company _____

Address _____

City/State/Zip _____

Phone _____

E-mail _____

☐ I am interested in AMA Membership so I can save on every seminar.

☐ I would like to receive AMA's monthly e-newsletter.

ATTN: CUSTOMER SERVICE

BUSINESS REPLY MAIL
FIRST-CLASS MAIL   PERMIT NO. 7172   NEW YORK, NY

POSTAGE WILL BE PAID BY ADDRESSEE

American Management Association
600 AMA WAY
SARANAC LAKE NY 12983-9963